PARIS

- A in the text denotes a highly recommended sight
- A complete A–Z of practical information starts on p.115
- Extensive mapping throughout: on cover flaps and in text

Printed in Switzerland by Weber SA, Bienne.

3rd edition (1996)

Although we make every effort to ensure the accuracy of the information in this guide, changes do occur. If you have any new information, suggestions or corrections to contribute, we would like to hear from you. Please write to Berlitz Publishing at one of the above addresses.

Text:	Martin Gostelow
Editors:	Renée Ferguson, Peter Duncan
Photography:	Pete Bennett
Layout:	Suzanna Boyle
Cartography:	Visual Image
Thanks to:	Giles Allen, Jack Altman; Eurostar for their assistance in the preparation of this guide.

Front cover photograph: *glass pyramid, Louvre*
Back cover photograph: *clock in Musée d'Orsay*
Photograph on page 4: *Rue Coquillière*

CONTENTS

Paris and the Parisians

It's no surprise that visitors flock to Paris. Where else can rival its combination of qualities? Magnificent monuments resonate with the echoes of a turbulent past. World-famous museums display unique treasures, in settings to match. All the amenities of a great capital are concentrated in a city on a human scale.

Throughout the ages Paris has always sent out seductive signals to the rest of the world: political freedom, sexual licence, revolutions in the arts, wonderful food, shops brimming with the good things of life. There were times not so long ago when the truth didn't match the myth. But not now. The art collections are as stunning, the shopping as enticing, the night life as varied as you could wish for, with streets as crowded at two o'clock in the morning as at midday.

Opera and ballet are both world class – the one staged in the modern Opéra-Bastille, the other in the finely restored 19th-century opera house. The jazz scene is vibrant, and other music from Algerian to Congolese finds the city a better showcase than its own homeland. Cinema is still accorded the status of an art – not only are the latest international releases shown, but laws also require a high percentage of home-grown productions to be screened on television and in the cinemas, keeping the local film industry busy in comparison with the rest of Europe.

A melting pot of people and cultures, France's capital has, surprisingly enough, no cuisine it can call its own – which doesn't matter because it can offer the pick of the regional dishes. Interpreted by today's creative chefs, French cuisine is lighter, brighter, fresher and tastier than ever. And if you want a change you'll find plenty of alternatives among the wide range of ethnic and foreign restaurants.

Take a seat at a café terrace and watch the world go by – at its pace or yours. The coffee or **5**

*P*aris diversions: take a cruise on the Seine at sunset, or kick up your heels in the street.

beer costs more than at the counter, but there's lots to see. Every passer-by seems to be giving a performance. Style is everything to Parisians, confident that they and their city are the centre of the universe and the focus of general admiration, not to say envy. A sometimes aloof exterior conceals a sensitive soul, caustic for sure, but alert and ready to engage in the battle of wits. To call someone an intellectual in France is still a compliment; philosophy, art and social issues provide the mainstay of many a café conversation.

Just who is 'the Parisian'? With a population of over two million, only one in two is actually born in the capital. Most hail from the provinces, from Brittany, Burgundy or Corsica – adding different ingredients to the Paris 'stew' – and within a few years they are Parisian

through and through, showing disdain for 'provincials' (who return the compliment), while remaining fiercely loyal to the province they left. Successive waves of refugees have also found a home here and left their marks: Jews, Armenians, Russians after 1917 – not all of them aristocrats – and Spanish Republicans during their Civil War. More recently have come large immigrant populations from north and west Africa and French territories in the Caribbean. No-one denies that there are problems of assimilation. It can only be hoped that time will gradually allay them.

Paris has not only restored buildings and built new structures, but it has altered its image too. It is now a clean city. Battalions of green-clad men and women and fleets of futuristic machines see to that. And yes, the plumbing works. You can go for days without meeting one of the famously surly waiters, shop assistants or taxi drivers of the past. Service with a smile is the motto in restaurants and shops these days. There's scarcely a hotel that hasn't been recently renovated, a public building that hasn't been scrubbed. Fresh paint and new gilding shines

wherever you look. Of course, there is another side to the coin: the usual big city afflictions of high unemployment, beggars in the métro and people without a home living in cardboard boxes.

When former President Mitterrand launched a programme of dramatic new building projects in 1981, he took the view that the state had an important role to play in the development of the capital. In doing so he was continuing in the tradition of several earlier French leaders. François I, Henri IV, Louis XIV and Napoleon all contributed to Paris' harmonious blend of styles. Napoleon III's arch-planner Haussmann cut ruthlessly through the old medieval maze of streets to give the city the wide avenues and boulevards that define its appearance to this day. Good luck or good management allowed Paris to miss out on the fad for high-rises. Only the Montparnasse skyscraper disturbs the near skyline: the towers and Grande Arche of La Défense draw the eye to the distant horizon without being obtrusive. The Pompidou Centre, Forum des Halles and Opéra-Bastille all caused bitter controversy, but in different ways brought new dynamism to a faded environment.

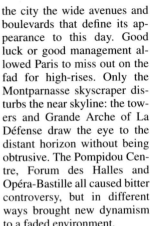

Each of the 20 *arrondissements*, or districts (see p.24), has its own character. Ethnic groups lend an exotic air to one street, while the next harbours the discreet apartments of the ultra-rich. A stately avenue spawns a tangle of little streets. Former working-class areas have become the height of chic, upstaging some formerly chic areas which have slid into decline. Villages that were absorbed as Paris developed have retained their individuality, their little shops and country-style markets.

The Left Bank remains distinct from the Right, despite a gradual fudging at the seams. Publishing houses and many art galleries and bookshops lie on the Left, the *rive gauche*, the intellectuals' bank, while the Right Bank has always attracted the Establishment: big names in fashion and cuisine, banks, offices and grand hotels. But it isn't that simple. Since in general French hearts lie on the Left and their wallets on the Right, many have a foot in both camps. So galleries and fashion houses often have branches on both banks, catering to their respective clienteles. Before and after World War II the young made a beeline for the Left Bank, leaving the Right to the rich and the 'Philistines', but now evenings can be far livelier around the transformed Les Halles, Beaubourg and Bastille than in the boulevards or lanes of Saint-Germain and Montparnasse.

When to visit Paris depends on your own preference and time. Each season has its distinct charms. A Parisian winter is nothing to dread; indeed, the

A sense of style is a Paris hallmark, whether at a fashion show (left) or in a city window.

classical façades seem to look their best under a cold, crisp light. Golden autumn holds as much romance as spring, when just a hint of sunshine brings café tables spilling out onto the terraces, the gardens come to life and love is in the air. In the heat of August half of Paris takes off on holiday and many restaurants close.

Whenever you choose to go you can watch life, window shop or just wander – there's always something happening. **9**

A Brief History

Origins

Defence came first, beauty simply followed. A Celtic tribe called the Parisii settled on an island in the River Seine, the present Ile de la Cité, around 300BC. Lutetia (marshland), as it was known, developed into a prosperous town, even issuing its own gold coins. The river, far wider than now, protected it against most invaders, but not the Romans, who took it in 52BC during Julius Caesar's conquest of Gaul.

The Right Bank of the river was too marshy to live on, so the town expanded to the Left Bank, in the area of the present Latin Quarter. In their customary fashion, the Romans built temples, straight roads, markets and bridges. The massive remains of their public baths still stand, right opposite the Sorbonne (see p.89). St Denis brought Christianity to the city and was rewarded by decapitation on the hill of Montmartre in around 250AD. Legend and popular depictions of the event have Denis picking up his head and walking away with it.

Towards the close of the third century, much of Roman Gaul was overrun by Germanic tribes of Huns and Franks, but Lutetia shrank back to the fortified Ile de la Cité and held out. In 486, by now known as Paris, the city fell to Clovis, king of the Franks. He became a convert to Christianity, and several religious foundations date from this time. The Left Bank was occupied once again and the church of Saint-Germain-des-Prés built there in the sixth century.

A Capital is Born

Though technically the main town of France (a region then much smaller than it is today), Paris wasn't sufficiently armed or organized to fight off the Vikings who, from 861, plundered it at regular intervals. It remained a backwater on the European scene until Hugues Capet, Count of Paris, was elected King of France in 987. Under the Capetian dynasty,

Historical landmarks

ca 300BC Celtic settlement on island in the River Seine.

52BC Roman conquest, followed by expansion to Left Bank.

486 Paris falls to Franks led by Clovis.

987 Hugues Capet elected King of France.

ca 1200 Building of Notre-Dame cathedral.

1420 English occupy Paris.

1431 Henry VI of England crowned King of France.

1436 English expelled.

1594 Henri IV enters Paris.

1682 Louis XIV moves court to Versailles.

1789 French Revolution.

1793 Execution of Louis XVI and Marie Antoinette. Reign of Terror.

1804 Napoleon becomes emperor.

1814 Fall of Napoleon. Restoration of Bourbon monarchy.

1815 Brief return of Napoleon (known as The 100 Days)

1830 'Bourgeois revolution'. Louis-Philippe, the Citizen King.

1848 Revolution brings Louis-Napoleon to power.

1870 Franco-Prussian War. Second Empire ends. Paris besieged.

1871 Paris Commune – brief period of workers' rule.

1900 First Métro line opened.

1914-18 World War I. Germans threaten Paris.

1939-45 World War II.

1940 French government capitulates. Germans occupy Paris.

1944 Free French and other Allied forces liberate Paris.

1958 Fall of Fourth Republic. De Gaulle becomes president.

1968 Student riots and demonstrations.

1973 Périphérique ring road completed, running around Paris.

1977 Jacques Chirac becomes first elected mayor since 1871.

1995 Jacques Chirac elected president.

Paris grew to be the economic and political capital. Its merchants exploited the commerce of the Seine and brought prosperity to the city, hence its old motto, *Fluctuat nec mergitur* (It has its ups and downs but doesn't sink), and the ship on its flag. The port area, known as the Grève, developed on the Right Bank by the present-day Châtelet and Hôtel de Ville. (To this day, the French for 'on strike' is *en grève*.)

Revenues from river trade financed the lengthy building of Notre-Dame, and enabled Philippe Auguste (1180-1223) to construct a fortress named the Louvre, as well as various aqueducts, fresh-water fountains and paved streets. To protect his investment while away on the Third Crusade (1189-1192), he surrounded the city with walls.

Louis IX (1226-70, canonized 1297) developed the spiritual and intellectual side of Paris, building the Gothic masterpiece, the Sainte-Chapelle, and many colleges on the Left Bank. In time they evolved into a university which took its name from one of them, La Sorbonne, established by the chaplain to the king, Robert de Sorbon. By the end of Louis' reign, Paris had become one of the greatest cities in Western Christendom, with a population of 100,000.

In the 14th century, plague (or the 'Black Death') and the

The Roman baths at Musée National du Moyen Age are a sign of the city's early past.

Hundred Years' War with England drained France. In 1356, with King Jean le Bon taken prisoner at Poitiers, the leader of the Paris merchants, Etienne Marcel, took advantage of the resulting confusion and set up a municipal dictatorship. Though assassinated two years later, Marcel had shown that the Parisians were a force to be reckoned with. Wary of their militancy, the subsequent king, Charles V, constructed the Bastille fortress.

If the 14th century had been unsettling for Paris, the 15th century opened even more disastrously. In 1407, the Duke of Burgundy had the Duke of Orleans murdered on the Rue Barbette, leading to 12 years of strife between their supporters. The Burgundians called in the help of the English, who entered Paris in 1420. Ten years later, Joan of Arc tried and failed to liberate the city, and the following year came worse humiliation: the young English King Henry VI was crowned King of France in Notre-Dame Cathedral. However, the English triumph was short-lived: they were soon expelled from the city, and by 1453 had lost all their French possessions but Calais.

Royal Patrons

With François I (1515-47), the city learned to thrive under an absolutist and absent monarch, busy with wars in Italy and even a year's imprisonment in Spain. The arts, sciences and literature flourished. Much of the Louvre was torn down and rebuilt along the present lines. A new Hôtel de Ville (town hall) was begun, as well as the superb Saint-Eustache church. Parisians were already assuming their distinctive pride in the uniqueness of their city. The poet Villon sang: *Il n'y a bon bec que de Paris* (only Parisians have real wit), while Pierre de Ronsard recorded a view of Paris as 'the city imbued with the discipline and glory of the muses'.

Bloody religious wars later wreaked havoc and mayhem, starting in 1572 with the infamous St Bartholomew's Day massacre of 3,000 Protestants **13** in Paris and culminating in the siege of the city by Henri de Navarre in 1589. Before the Catholic League capitulated, 13,000 Parisians had died of starvation. Henri was crowned at Chartres and finally entered the capital in 1594 – but not before he had turned Catholic himself, noting famously (and ambiguously) that 'Paris is well worth a mass'.

Henri IV did Paris proud once he was its master. He built the beautiful Place des Vosges and Place Dauphine, embellished the banks of the river with the Quais de l'Arsenal, de l'Horloge and des Orfèvres, and even constructed the Samaritaine hydraulic machine that pumped fresh water to Right Bank households up until 1813. Most popular of France's monarchs, *le bon roi Henri* (good King Henry) was also a notorious ladies' man. He completed the Pont-Neuf (the oldest bridge in Paris) as well as the adjacent gardens, where he was known to dally with his ladies.

During the reign of Louis XIII (1610-43), Paris began to

The early 17th-century Place des Vosges remains one of the most beautiful squares in Paris.

take on the fashionable aspect that became its hallmark. Elegant houses sprang up along the Rue du Faubourg-Saint-Honoré, and the magnificent *hôtels* (mansions) of the nobility mushroomed in the Marais. The capital consolidated its growing position as the hub of the country with the establishment of a royal printing press, the Académie Française of Cardinal Richelieu, and in gaining ecclesiastical status as an archbishopric.

Paris increasingly attracted nobles from the provinces – too much so for the liking of Louis XIV, *le roi Soleil* (the Sun King – 1643-1715). To bring his overly powerful and independent aristocrats back into line, he decided to move the court out of the capital to Versailles, compelling them to live at vast expense in his enormous new palace. Paris lost

most of its political clout, but looked more impressive than ever with the landscaping of the Tuileries Gardens and the Champs-Elysées, the building of the Louvre's great colonnade and the Invalides hospital for wounded and retired soldiers. The city continued to assert its cultural ascendancy with the organization of the new academies of the arts, literature and sciences and the establishment of the Comédie-Française (1680) and several other theatres. The population increased to 560,000, almost six times as many as in the 13th century.

The Sun King's successors, the indolent Louis XV (1715-74) and the inept Louis XVI, became increasingly unpopular, even hated, as corruption ruled and their ministers tried to raise taxes to pay for costly foreign wars. One of the final construction projects of the *ancien régime* (the old, or pre-revolutionary regime) was a new 23km (14-mile) wall running around the perimeter of the city. Begun in 1784, this became a major factor in the coming unrest, for it was along the wall that taxes were collected on the various goods brought into the city.

Revolution

The 1789 French Revolution was not the first to break out in Paris, nor the last, nor even the bloodiest, but its effects were the most far-reaching. Starting with protests by the gentry about taxes, it was taken up by the middle classes (the *bourgeoisie*) who wanted to cut the

The story of the Revolution that turned the world upside down is told at the Musée Carnavalet.

privileges of the monarchy, aristocracy and church. And it was middle class intellectuals who then stirred up the urban poor, the previously powerless *sans-culottes* (people without breeches) to revolt.

A climax was reached on 21 January 1793, with the public beheading of Louis XVI in the Place de la Révolution, nowadays called Place de la Concorde. In the Reign of Terror later that year (Year I of the new calendar), many perceived enemies of the new republic followed him to the guillotine.

Several were revolutionaries themselves: Desmoulins the fiery orator and Danton who tried to moderate the Terror, and then the men who had organized it, Robespierre and Saint-Just.

In 1799, Napoleon Bonaparte imposed his authority as effective dictator, and later as Emperor. Frequent absences on foreign business did not hinder his projects for making Paris the capital of Europe. Detailed maps of the city and architectural plans for new buildings never left his side. Visitors can see Napoleon's mark in spectacular monuments – the Arc de Triomphe and the column of the Grande-Armée on the Place Vendôme – but the Emperor himself was proudest of his civic improvements: fresh water in quantity throughout the city, improved drainage, new food markets, a streamlined municipal administration and police force. The majority of his reforms survived his fall in 1814 and final defeat the following year, and became a model for modern urban government.

The monarchy returned, but the concentration in Paris of an ambitious bourgeoisie, dissatisfied workers and radical intellectuals was an ever-present threat. In July 1830, protest turned to riots and the building of barricades. Charles X, who in the Bourbon tradition had 'forgotten nothing and learned nothing' from history, was forced to abdicate. But instead of restoring the republic, the revolutionary leaders played safe and agreed to the accession of the moderate Louis-Philippe, the 'Citizen King'.

The Revolution of 1848, which brought his 'bourgeois' monarchy to an end, likewise started with riots and barricades in the streets of Paris. A mob threatened the royal palace, forcing him to flee, and then invaded the Chamber of Deputies demanding a republic. Elections followed, but they showed that however radical Paris might be, the rest of France was still largely conservative. The new National Assembly withdrew the concessions that had been made to the workers; and up went the **17** barricades again. This time the army was called in with its heavy guns. At least 1500 insurrectionists were killed, and thousands deported.

A new democratic system was adopted and it might have worked, but in voting for a president the people voted for a name, Louis-Napoleon, the nephew of the dead Emperor. In 1851 he seized absolute power, and the next year became Emperor Napoleon III. (The second of the line, son of the first, never reigned and died young.)

Capital Facelift

It was fear that led Napoleon III to modernize Paris. The insurrections of 1830 and 1848 had flared up in the densely populated working-class districts around the centre and he wanted to prevent any chance of a recurrence. He therefore commissioned Baron Georges Haussmann to do away with the clusters of narrow streets and alleys that nurtured discontent. The baron razed them and moved the occupants out to the suburbs, creating the 'red belt' which makes Paris one of the few Western capitals whose suburbs are not predominantly conservative. This ruthless approach made way for a 'new' Paris, far removed from the old in looks and spirit, but with its own charm.

Broad boulevards and avenues highlighted the monuments, churches and public buildings. As the baron explained to his emperor, these avenues were too wide for barricades and gave the artillery a clear line of fire in case of revolt. But this Second Empire was also a time of joyous abandon and boisterous expansion. World fairs in 1855 and 1867 drew royalty from England, Russia and Prussia, eager to view the 'gay Paree' depicted in Offenbach's operettas.

After a foolish declaration of war against Prussia in 1870, the army of Napoleon III was quickly defeated. His disgrace and capture brought the proclamation of a new republic, followed by a crippling siege of Paris by the Prussians. The city held out, though reduced to starvation level, and communicated with the rest of the country by means of balloons (bearing pigeons to bring messages back). When France's leaders agreed to peace, there was yet another uprising. The Paris Commune (self-rule by the workers) lasted 10 weeks, from 18 March to 29 May 1871, until Adolphe Thiers, first president of the Third Republic, sent in troops from Versailles to crush it. The *communards* were pushed back street by street and in the last days set fire to buildings such as the Tuileries Palace, and executed hostages including the Archbishop of Paris. The government took its vengeance: at least 20,000 Commune supporters were killed in the fighting or executed afterwards.

Ups and Downs

In spite of the horrors of siege and civil war, prosperity rapidly returned and the capital's resurrection was marked by a great construction boom. Projects begun under Napoleon III, such as the opera house and the huge Les Halles market, were completed. Star of the show was the Eiffel Tower (built in 1889), as techniques using iron improved beyond all recognition. By the end of the 19th century, the splendid new *métro* began to provide fast and comfortable transport across the city.

Artists, writers and revolutionaries flocked to this hub of creative activity. Picasso came over from Barcelona in 1900, followed by Modigliani from Livorno, Soutine from Minsk, Stravinsky from St Petersburg and Gertrude Stein from San Francisco. Then ensued a long stream of American artists and writers led by Ernest Hemingway and F. Scott Fitzgerald.

Two wars, of course, took their toll. The Germans threatened but failed to take Paris during World War I, but they occupied it for four long and unhappy years (1940-44) during World War II. Liberation came eventually, with a parade by General de Gaulle and his Free French forces down the Champs-Elysées. Unlike many great European capitals, Paris **19**

ICI EST TOMBÉ
POUR LA LIBÉRATION DE PARIS
LE 22 AOÛT 1944
ROGER LAMBERT
ÂGÉ DE 19 ANS

Some who fought against the occupation did not live to see the Liberation. The others remember.

was never bombed, and Hitler's vengeful order to burn it before retreating had mercifully been ignored. After World War II, recovery was slow as governments came and went in rapid succession. The Fourth Republic died, unregretted, in 1958, following an army revolt at the time of the colonial war in Algeria. Recalled from retirement, General de Gaulle thus became the first president of the Fifth Republic and set about restoring French prestige and morale.

Modern Times

In May 1968 Parisian students and workers recaptured some of the old revolutionary spirit. Walls were daubed with slogans and the Latin Quarter's paving stones were hurled at the smugly entrenched Establishment. But national elections showed that, as so often in the past, Paris was at odds with most of France which voted for stability. Succeeding de Gaulle, Georges Pompidou picked up the pieces and affirmed the new prosperity with riverside expressways and skyscrapers, and the controversial but hugely successful Beaubourg cultural centre which bears his name.

In 1977 Jacques Chirac became the first democratically elected mayor of Paris. (For more than a century, since the stormy days of the Commune, the national government controlled the city through its own appointed officials.) In a country where politicians are allowed to double as mayor and prime minister, Parisians benefit from leaders keen to further their national political ambitions with a dynamic municipal performance. Chirac made the most of his opportunity, and took the credit for the effective clean-up of the formerly dirty, shabby streets.

Former President François Mitterrand made his own mark on the Paris skyline with a series of innovative and impressive works: the Grande Arche, the Opéra-Bastille, the Institut du Monde Arabe and a whole project to reorganize the Louvre around a great glass pyramid. Some were timed for completion in 1989, when the 200th anniversary of the Revolution was celebrated in style.

Jacques Chirac at last relinquished the mayor's job when he was himself elected president in 1995, the culmination of a persistent 20-year campaign. Poised on the eve of the 21st century, Paris has probably never looked better. Monuments shine with fresh layers of gold leaf, new and remodelled museums display its heritage and it continues to wield an astonishing cultural influence throughout the world. **21**

What to See

GETTING AROUND

As soon as you can, buy a Museum Pass (see p.88) to save money and avoid waiting at ticket desks; and a book of 10 métro tickets (good for buses too) or, better still, one of the special deals which give even greater savings (see p.134).

To get your bearings, picture Paris as a circle, with the river Seine threading across the centre, flanked by famous landmarks – Notre-Dame, the Louvre, Place de la Concorde, the Eiffel Tower. Bridges of all shapes and sizes tie the Right (north) and Left Banks together or link them to the two islands in the middle, Ile de la Cité and Ile Saint-Louis.

This is one of the easiest of large cities to get about. The modernized **métro** system is smooth, regular and fast, with low, flat-rate fares. **RER** commuter trains can also take you rapidly to places on the outskirts. **Buses** give you a sightseeing tour at a bargain price, while adhering to schedules as far as traffic allows (rush hours can create terrible jams). **Taxis** provide a lazy alternative.

Bus tours take you to the big attractions, but inevitably at times when they are busiest. Some tour buses which take you round the highlights let you hop on and off, wherever and as often as you like, all on one ticket, for a period of up to 48 hours. Tourist information offices (see p.133) have details. **Bicycle** hire companies (see p.117) also run tours. If you want to do it in style (and expensively) you can even see Paris from a helicopter, plane or hot-air balloon.

A **boat** cruise on the Seine is one of the best introductions to the city. While you glide along, multilingual commentaries tell you about the sights. Boats run from about 10am to 10.30pm. Most tour boats provide a choice of open-air and glassed-in seating, some offer lunch and dinner, and trips last 60-75 minutes. Canal tours reveal a less grand face of Paris on the way from the centre to Parc de la Villette (see p.87) in the north-eastern suburbs. The trip takes three hours, with a 2km (1.2 mile) tunnel and several locks to be negotiated.

Parisians themselves often use the *Bat-O-Bus* (river bus) for travelling east or west and avoiding traffic snarls. It runs from May to September; stops are at the Eiffel Tower, Musée d'Orsay, Louvre, Notre-Dame and Hôtel de Ville. It's expensive, but you may prefer the absence of commentary.

Central Paris is surprisingly compact and most hotels are close to many of the sights. So if time isn't a major factor, the best way of getting the feel of the place is to **walk**. All you need is a pair of comfortable shoes and a **map**. The big department stores and hotels give away millions of street maps each year. Métro stations display good maps of their local district as well as the métro itself, and give out pocket plans of the métro and bus routes. More and more streets and entire areas like Les Halles and Beaubourg have been pedestrianized, adding to the profusion of parks, squares and gardens.

*T*he signs may be antique, but the métro is modern and quick. Cruises are a restful alternative. **23**

Paris by numbers

The city is divided into 20 districts or *arrondissements*, the numbers spiralling outwards like a snail's shell, starting at the centre around the Louvre. When Parisians refer to the 5th (*cinquième*), or 16th (*seizième*), for example, they have a clear image of the sorts of shop, restaurant, housing and people to be found there.

Most of the places you'll be visiting are in numbers 1-9, with a few forays further out. Here's an idea of the way the districts divide:

1er: the Louvre to Les Halles, and half of Ile de la Cité.

2e: south of the *grands boulevards*; financial district, many theatres.

3e: quiet, old streets of the northern Marais.

4e: Pompidou Centre to southern Marais; Jewish quarter.

5e: Latin Quarter; educational institutions and student life.

6e: Saint-Germain-des-Prés; intellectuals, bookshops, restaurants.

7e: Musée d'Orsay to the Eiffel Tower; elegant apartments.

8e: Champs-Elysées to Madeleine; luxury shops, fashion houses.

9e: Opéra-Garnier and big department stores.

10e: Gare du Nord; not many sights; walks along Canal St. Martin.

11e: Bastille; once poor, now trendy; galleries, night-life.

12e: bordering on Bois de Vincennes; nearby zoo.

13e: tower blocks; large Far Eastern community.

14e: Montparnasse; commercial development, cafés.

15e: Rue de Vaugirard (Paris' longest street); food markets.

16e: Arc de Triomphe to Bois de Boulogne; expensive housing.

17e: residential chic; food shops on Rue Lévis.

18e: Montmartre; village life and low life.

19e and 20e: Père Lachaise, Belleville; poor suburbs and La Villette.

Street numbering follows a rough pattern too. The lower numbers are generally nearest the Seine, with evens on the right and odds on the left as you move 'inland'. Streets parallel to the river are numbered in an upstream-downstream direction.

The Islands

ILE DE LA CITE

Fittingly for the cradle of a town that grew from its river commerce, the Ile de la Cité is shaped like a boat, with the green, shaded **Square du Vert Galant** pointing downstream. From the first settlement built by the original Parisii until the middle of the 19th century, the pocket-sized island lay at the heart of the city. The heavy-handed Baron Haussmann (see p.18) then swept away virtually all the medieval and 17th-century structures, leaving just Place Dauphine and Rue Chanoinesse (the ancient home of the cathedral canons) as signs of the island's once rich residential life.

The baron was also toying with the idea of replacing the gracious red-brick houses of the triangular Place Dauphine with a neo-Grecian colonnaded square when, thankfully, he was forced out of office for juggling the books. Near the lively **Pont-Neuf**, the *place*

(square) was built in 1607 by Henri IV in honour of his son the *dauphin* (or future king, Louis XIII). Sadly, only numbers 14 and 26 are still in their original state.

The huge **Palais de Justice**, heart of the centralized French legal system, stands on the site of the Roman palace where the Emperor Julian was crowned in 360. Together with the Conciergerie (see p.26), it sprawls right across the Ile de la Cité. Concealed in the courtyard between them is a Gothic masterpiece, the **Sainte-Chapelle**, whose fine proportions stand in sharp contrast to the ponderous palace. The chapel was constructed in 1248 to house holy relics, Christ's Crown of Thorns and a fragment of the True Cross, which the pious Louis IX (later canonized as St Louis) had bought from the Byzantine emperor. If you can, arrive as the chapel opens (see p.35) and make your way to the upper level, where light blazes in through 15 stained-glass windows separated by buttresses so slim that there seems to be no wall at all. **25**

Miraculously, of the 1,134 individual pieces of glass, 720 are 13th-century originals. On the odd occasion, concerts are held here: such a setting could hardly be bettered.

Between 1789 and 1815 the chapel assumed various guises: a flour warehouse during the Revolution and a club for high-ranking dandies, then an archive for Napoleon's Consulate. It was this latter role that saved the chapel from projected destruction, since the bureaucrats could not think of another site to put their mountains of paper.

These days, they find room in the Palais de Justice and the nearby **Préfecture de Police**, haunt of those fictional detectives, Inspectors Maigret and Clouseau. The great lobby of the Palais, the Salle des Pas Perdus is worth a visit for a glimpse of the many lawyers, plaintiffs, witnesses, court reporters and assorted hangers-on waiting nervously for the wheels of French justice to grind into action.

Their anxiety is as nothing compared with that of the prisoners once held in the forbidding **Conciergerie** – reached from the Quai de l'Horloge. Part of the 14th-century royal palace, it was probably named after the *Compte des Cierges* (Count of the Candles), who was traditionally in charge of punishments; slowly it took on the role of a prison. In 1793, at

Once a prison, the Conciergerie now looks quietly over the Seine and Pont au Change.

Bridges of Paris

Within the city, no fewer than 36 bridges span the Seine. Whether you are walking or riding, there are some that you'll use frequently, and they're a big feature of the river cruises.

Pont-Neuf (new bridge) is in fact the oldest survivor, dating from 1606, the reign of Henri IV – seen on horseback at the centre. It was kept free of the houses that lined earlier bridges, and soon became, and still is, a popular place to meet and stroll. Some of the hawkers, musicians, pickpockets and tooth-pullers who used to gather here are caricatured in grimacing stone heads on the cornice facing the river.

Pont des Arts is the next downstream, a spidery iron structure also reserved for walkers and a favourite meeting point on the way to the Latin Quarter.

Pont-Royal crosses where the Louvre meets the Tuileries gardens and gives a great view of both, as well as the Musée d'Orsay on the other bank. It was built for Louis XIV in 1685.

Pont de la Concorde was started before the Revolution and completed in 1790, using stones from the dismantled Bastille. Its original name of Pont Louis XVI was duly changed to Pont de la Révolution the year before the king went to the guillotine nearby in Place de la Révolution (now Concorde).

Pont Alexandre III was named after the Tsar of Russia whose successor, Nicholas II, laid the first stone in 1896. It was the first bridge with a single steel arch, and the widest. The cast-iron lamp standards are characteristic of its era, the Belle Epoque, and gilded statues at the ends depict medieval and modern France (Right Bank), and France of the renaissance and Louis XIV (Left Bank).

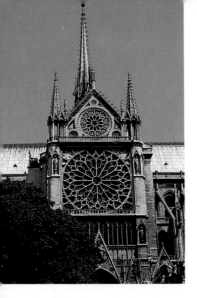

the condemned. About 2,500 victims of the Revolutionary guillotine spent their last hours in the Conciergerie.

Notre-Dame

The site of the Cathedral of Notre-Dame de Paris has had a religious role for at least 2,000 years. In Roman times a temple to Jupiter stood here; some stone fragments unearthed in 1711 can be seen in the Musée du Moyen Age (see p.86). In the 4th century, the first Christian church, Saint-Etienne, was built, joined two centuries later by a second church, dedicated to Notre Dame. Viking and Norman raids left both in a sorry state, and Bishop Maurice de Sully decided a cathedral should be built to replace them. Begun in 1163, the main part of Notre-Dame took no less than 167 years to finish,

the height of the Terror, it was literally the 'antechamber of the guillotine'. Queen Marie-Antoinette, Robespierre, Danton and Saint-Just all spent their last nights in the Galerie des Prisonniers. The Salle des Girondins displays a guillotine blade, the crucifix to which Marie-Antoinette prayed and the lock used on Robespierre's cell. Look out on the Cour des Femmes, where husbands, lovers, wives and mistresses were allowed one final tryst before **28** the tumbrels came to carry off and thus spanned the transition from Romanesque to Gothic.

The cathedral has been the setting for numerous momentous occasions: in 1239 Louis IX walked barefoot through it with his holy treasure, the Crown of Thorns (before the Sainte-Chapelle was built); in 1430 it saw Henry VI of England crowned King of France (see p.13); in 1594 Henri IV attended the mass that sealed his conversion to Catholicism and reinforced his hold on the French throne. Here in 1804, Napoleon crowned himself as Emperor, upstaging the Pope who had come to Paris expecting to do it. More recently, the cathedral held the state funerals of heroes such as Foch, Leclerc and de Gaulle.

Across the three doorways of the west front, the 28 statues of the **Galerie des Rois** represent the kings of Judah. These are 19th-century restorations: the originals were torn down during the Revolution because they were thought to depict kings of France (a number are preserved in the Musée du Moyen Age, see p.86). The superb central **rose window** depicts the Redemption after the Fall: the view of it from the inside is partly blocked by the huge organ. Two more outsize rose windows illuminate the transept; the northern window, incredibly, retains most of its 13th-century glass. Don't miss the 14th-century **Virgin and Child** that bears the cathedral's name, Notre-Dame de Paris (Our Lady of Paris), to the right of the choir entrance.

*T*he flower market at Place Lepine on Ile de la Cité switches to selling cage birds on Sunday. **29**

The original architect of the Cathedral of Notre-Dame is unknown, but Pierre de Montreuil (who was involved in the building of Sainte-Chapelle)

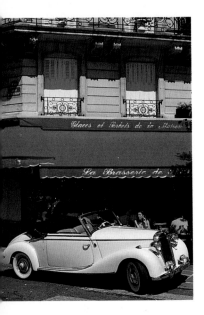

*I*t sometimes seems as if time has stood still in the quiet streets of Ile Saint-Louis.

30

was responsible for a large part of the 13th-century work. The present state of the cathedral owes a great deal to Eugène Viollet-le-Duc, who laboured patiently from 1845 to 1863 to restore it following the ravages of the 18th century, caused by pre-Revolutionary meddlers as well as the Revolutionaries who stripped it of its religious symbols and declared it a Temple of Reason.

The long climb up the **north tower** may be strenuous (there are 245 steps), but the wonderful views of Paris and close-ups of the roof and gargoyles make it well worth the effort. Once up there, you can cross to the south tower to see the 13-tonne bell, the only one remaining – the Revolutionaries melted down all the others to make cannon. It was re-cast in the 1680s but the story that its bronze was mixed with gold and silver donated by Louis XIV's nobles appears to be a myth, although perhaps their contributions paid for it. A further 124 steps lead to the top of the south tower for still more spectacular views.

Baron Haussmann greatly enlarged the *parvis*, or square, in front of the cathedral, diminishing the impact of its towering west front. Photographers may appreciate the view he created, but early photographs show what was lost. You'll find some of them on display in the **crypt** beneath the square. The result of an archaeological dig which revealed walls and foundations from the Gallic, Roman and medieval eras, the crypt was roofed over so that the ruins could remain on show in a brilliantly designed exhibition on early Paris.

ILE SAINT-LOUIS

Though connected by a bridge, the sister islands are far apart in spirit. The Ile Saint-Louis, formed by joining and draining two mudbanks in the 17th century, is a sanctuary of gracious living, its quiet streets lined by elegant houses and mansions, where rich artists, politicians, doctors, actresses and heiresses have lived. President Pompidou had a house on the Quai de Béthune and used to escape there from the Elysée Palace as frequently as he could.

The most striking of the mansions, the **Hôtel Lauzun**, at 17 Quai d'Anjou, was built in the 1650s by Le Vau, who also worked on the Seine façade of the Louvre and the Versailles château. The **Hôtel Lambert**, another very impressive mansion designed by Le Vau for the Sun King's secretary, stands on the corner of the Rue Saint-Louis-en-l'Ile. Voltaire once enjoyed a tempestuous love affair here with the lady of the house, the marquise du Châtelet. The church of **Saint-Louis-en-l'Ile** is airy and bright, and a golden light illuminates a good collection of Dutch, Flemish and Italian 16th- and 17th-century art.

From the western end of the shady Quai d'Orléans, you'll have a splendid view of the apse of Notre-Dame, although the majority of pilgrims to this spot are more intent on a visit to Berthillon, the celebrated maker of ice creams and delicious sorbets.

Right Bank

From ultra-chic to downright sleazy, the Right Bank (*rive droite*) covers the most fashionable shopping areas, the presidential Elysée Palace, the *grands boulevards* and financial district and, further north, seamy Clichy and Pigalle, and hilly Montmartre where modern art could be said to have begun. Back in the middle of it all, the enormous Louvre museum stands as a magnificent challenge, and just to the east of the central area, Les Halles, Beaubourg (around the Pompidou Centre) and Place de la Bastille have each been transformed by controversial projects: the variety and energy of their night-life has overtaken that of the Left Bank. Half forgotten and thereby saved from such schemes, the charming old Marais and Jewish quarter preserve the old Paris of the 17th century.

We start at a commanding landmark and symbol of the city and nation.

PLACE CHARLES-DE-GAULLE (L'ETOILE)

Known as the Place de l'Etoile until the death of Charles de Gaulle in 1969, this great circular space with its whirling traffic is dominated by the vast **Arc de Triomphe**, (50m high and 45m wide, or 164ft by 148ft). A trip to the top by elevator, or around 300 steps, is worth the high price – not a factor if you have invested in a Museum Pass (see p.88) – for the spectacular view. The star (*l'Etoile*) is formed by 12 avenues radiating outwards in a tour de force of geometric planning which cannot really be taken in at ground level.

Grandiose and not a little absurd, the Arc de Triomphe was conceived by Napoleon I as a tribute to his armies, and bears the names of hundreds of his marshals and generals, and dozens of victories. No defeats are recorded, naturally, although a few of the victories are debatable (some appearing on British battle honours too). Napoleon himself only ever saw a wood and canvas model: the arch was completed during the 1830s. It soon became the focus for state occasions such as the return of the ex-emperor's own remains from St Helena in 1840 and the funeral of Victor Hugo in 1885. In 1920, the Unknown Soldier of World War I was buried at the arch; three years later the eternal

*T*here's a fine view from the Arc de Triomphe (far left). Guard at the Elysée Palace (left).

flame was lit. When Adolf Hitler arrived in Paris as a conqueror in 1940, the Arc de Triomphe was the first place he wanted to see. And at the Liberation this was the spot where General de Gaulle commenced his triumphal march down the Champs-Elysées.

Avenue Foch, leading away from l'Etoile to the Bois de Boulogne, is one of the most majestic of the city's residential avenues. One of the most exclusive, too, though somewhat democratized these days by the groups of boules players on its gravelled side paths. Avenue de la Grande-Armée points straight to Neuilly and the towers of La Défense with the Grande Arche behind.

AVENUE DES CHAMPS-ELYSEES

It's fashionable nowadays to look down on the Champs-Elysées (Parisians may inform you they never set foot there), but despite extensive commercialization it remains one of the finest avenues anywhere in the world, straight as a rod,

sloping at a gentle pace down to the Place de la Concorde and fringed by chestnut trees, the object of careful replanting to ensure that it retains its elegant beauty.

The top two-thirds of the avenue are filled with cinemas, airline offices and car showrooms, the excellent **Tourist Information Office** (no 127), some shops and café terraces that make perfect, if slightly expensive, vantage points for people-watching.

Below the Rond-Point, the mood changes and a pleasant park leads you past two landmarks: the **Petit Palais**, all steel and glass, and the **Grand Palais**. Both were constructed for the Universal Exhibition of 1900 and are today used for a variety of exhibitions, though the Petit Palais houses several permanent collections of 19th-century French paintings. The Grand Palais shares its colossal building with the Palais de la Découverte (see p.89), and includes among its displays a hands-on exhibition of the sciences, with a planetarium as centre-piece.

Paris highlights

Arc de Triomphe. Honours Napoleon's armies and their victories. The view from the top is superb. Open 9.30am-11pm, Tuesday-Saturday, to 6.30pm Sunday, Monday (winter 10am-5pm daily). Métro: Charles de Gaulle-Etoile.

Eiffel Tower. The world's tallest structure when it was built in 1889, and still a marvel. Open daily 9.30am-11pm (July and August 9am-midnight). Métro: Bir-Hakeim, Ecole Militaire, Trocadéro.

La Défense. It's worth the métro trip to see this development and especially the Grande Arche. Open always. Grande Arche roof: open 9am-7pm (8pm Saturday, Sunday, holidays). Closes one hour earlier, October-March. Métro: Grande Arche de la Défense.

Les Halles. Formerly a food market, now a garden. The glitzy Forum des Halles shopping complex, partly below ground, is a teenagers' mecca. Open always. Shops: 10am-7pm, closed Sunday, Monday morning. Métro: Châtelet-Les Halles, Les Halles.

Invalides. A 17th-century army veterans' hospital, home to the Army Museum and Napoleon's tomb. Open: Museum 10am-6pm (5pm October-March); Napoleon's tomb 10am-6pm (7pm June-August, 5pm October-March). Métro: Latour-Maubourg, Invalides.

La Madeleine. A Greco-Roman temple on the outside and a magnificent church inside. Open 7.30am-7pm (Sunday 8am-1.30pm; 3.30-7pm). Métro: Madeleine.

Notre-Dame Cathedral. A masterpiece of early Gothic and the symbol of Paris for 800 years. The view from the towers is superb, and the crypt reveals the Roman foundations of the city. Open 8am-7pm (Saturday 8am-12.30pm, 2-7pm). Crypt 10am-6pm (5pm October-March). Métro: Cité, Maubert-Mutualité, Hôtel-de-Ville.

Sainte-Chapelle. A 13th-century jewel of Gothic architecture, with breathtaking stained glass. Open 9.30am-6.30pm (10am-5pm, October-March). Métro: Châtelet, Saint-Michel.

Place des Vosges. The heart of the Marais, an elegant square of matching houses, planned by Henri IV in 1605. Victor Hugo lived at no. 6, now a museum. Métro: St-Paul, Chemin-Vert.

his hands on during a campaign, but a gift from Mohammed Ali, viceroy of Egypt. The two imposing horses that watch over the opening to the Champs-Elysées are replicas of the great Chevaux de Marly, sculpted by Coustou between 1740 and 1745. (The marble originals now grace the Cour Marly of the Louvre.)

The expansive **Place de la Concorde** was designed by Jacques-Ange Gabriel as Place Louis XV in 1753, but the Revolution dispensed with all royal connotations. The king's statue was replaced by a guillotine, soon to be used to behead Louis XVI and more than 1000 other victims. In 1934 it was the scene of bloody rioting against the government; and ten years later it was the Nazis' last foothold in Paris.

Plumb in the centre, the 23m (75ft) pink granite Obelisk of Luxor from the temple of Ramses II dates back to 1300BC and was erected here in 1836. For a change, it's not **36** something that Napoleon laid

JARDIN DES TUILERIES

After the bustle of the Place de la Concorde and the Champs-Elysées, take refuge among the chestnut trees and Maillol's sensual statues in these gardens, named after a 13th-century tileworks. The impressive size of the gardens results from the burning down of the Palais des Tuileries during the 1871 Commune (see p.19); a few fragments can be seen by the Jeu de Paume exhibition building in the north-west corner. Children can enjoy donkey rides, puppet shows in spring and summer and model boats on the circular ponds.

In the corner near the Seine, facing Place de la Concorde,

the **Orangerie** is known for its two oval rooms with Monet's beautiful *Nymphéas* (water-lilies) murals, but don't miss the marvellous Impressionist and post-Impressionist paintings upstairs (see p.85).

At the eastern end of the Tuileries stands the pink **Arc de Triomphe du Carrousel**, started at roughly the same time but finished much more quickly than its bigger brother at l'Etoile, which is visible from here in a straight line beyond the obelisk in Place de la Concorde. The same axis continues into the distant haze to the skyscrapers of La Défense and the Grande Arche.

PALAIS DU LOUVRE

This is truly one of the world's treasure houses (see p.88 for information about visits, and p.81 for more about the contents). Its harmonious lines are deceptive: the Louvre has been eight centuries in the making. Ever since Philippe Auguste built a fortress in 1190 to protect Paris from attack along the river, kings and queens have added to it and altered it. Louis XIV more or less abandoned the Louvre when he moved the court to Versailles, and it was taken over by artists, sculptors and squatters. The Revolution-aries declared it to be a muse-um, and opened it to the public

*R*elax in the shade, or go for a spin: the big wheel is a summer fixture in the Tuileries gardens.

in 1793. As the home of the *Vénus de Milo* and *Mona Lisa*, the Louvre drew ever-greater crowds until by the beginning of the 1980s it was unable to cope. An enormous new reception area was excavated (revealing parts of the original fort). The controversial glass **pyramid** designed by I.M. Pei in the Cour Napoléon serves as its roof and focus.

The old church of **Saint-Germain l'Auxerrois** on the eastern side of the complex dates from around 1200, but like the palace, it was adapted many times, and often served as the royal chapel.

PALAIS-ROYAL

Across the Rue de Rivoli from the Louvre, the Palais-Royal was built as Cardinal Richelieu's residence in 1639 (it became 'royal' when Anne of Austria moved in with young Louis XIV). This serene, arcaded palace, with its garden of lime trees and beeches – and the pond where Louis XIV nearly drowned – has had a colourful past. In the days of Philippe d'Orléans, Regent of France while Louis XV was a child, the Palais-Royal was the scene of notorious orgies. A later duke (another Philippe) constructed apartments round

Seen from the little Arc de Triomphe du Carrousel, the pyramid marks the Louvre's main entrance.

the garden, with two theatres (one became the national Comédie Française), shops and cafés that soon attracted fashionable society. In the ferment that led up to the Revolution, it was the focus of furious debate. On 13 July 1789 a young firebrand orator, Camille Desmoulins, stood on a table at the Palais-Royal's Café de Foy to sound a call to arms. The Bastille was stormed the next day.

Giving himself the name Philippe Egalité (equality), the duke tried to curry favour with the Revolutionaries but was guillotined anyway. After the revolution, the palace became a gambling den again and narrowly escaped destruction in the 1871 uprising. Once it was restored, between 1872 and 1876, the palace became respectable and today houses the Council of State and the Constitutional Council. Some of the shops still exist, selling medals and antiques, and the sumptuously decorated Grand Véfour restaurant looks just the way it did 200 years ago.

The main quadrangle, the **Cour d'Honneur**, was filled in 1986 with rows of black and white striped stone columns by Daniel Buren. Some are short, some tall, a few are just the right height for sitting on.

Next to the Palais-Royal stand the **Banque de France**, east of the garden, and the **Bibliothèque Nationale** (National Library), just north of it. The idea of a royal library was born in 1368, when Charles V placed 973 manuscripts in the Louvre. Two centuries later, François I acquired new material, had Oriental, Latin and Greek texts copied and made it all available to scholars. He also ruled in 1573 that a copy of any work printed in France had to be given to the library. It has had to grow non-stop to house more than 10 million books, 12 million engravings, 650,000 maps and more than 350,000 ancient manuscripts, one of which is Charlemagne's *Evangéliaire*. A new building on the Left Bank just opposite Bercy, dubbed *Très Grande Bibliothèque* (Very Large Library), will gradually take over the role as books are moved over there. **39**

LES HALLES

East of the Palais-Royal, this was for centuries the site of the capital's central food markets (now in a more spacious if less colourful location at Rungis, near Orly). To widespread regret, the great cast-iron and glass pavilions were torn down in the 1970s. They were eventually replaced by today's gardens and play areas, and the **Forum des Halles**, a maze-like shopping mall partly below ground. Saturdays bring throngs of teenagers from the suburbs to shop, play video games, roller skate, munch fast food and generally hang out together. The liveliest meeting place in the area is the handsome Renaissance **Fontaine des Innocents** (once part of a cemetery). Bars, restaurants and 24-hour brasseries line the southern side, Rue Berger and the streets leading off it. Clubs and discos around here come alive at midnight and stay open to dawn, especially at weekends. It's not all innocent fun: drink and drugs mix with pickpockets and prostitutes. Rue Saint-Denis, once known primarily as a red-light district, is now pedestrianized and still has its share of sex shops.

The great church of **Saint-Eustache** dominates the north side of Les Halles. Built during the 16th and 17th centuries, the concept is late Gothic, the details are Renaissance, and the effect is awe-inspiring. Notice the sad modern shrine, with sculptures of the departing market traders, and the poem referring to a 'paradise lost'. If you are lucky, you may hear a recital on the splendid organ, or the choir rehearsing.

POMPIDOU CENTRE (BEAUBOURG)

East of the Forum, streets closed to traffic and lined with cafés, brasseries, art galleries and boutiques link up with the unusual Centre Georges Pompidou, housing the Musée National d'Art Moderne (for visit details, see p.88, and contents, p.85). Controversy raged for years after the 1977 opening of this multicoloured 'oil refinery'. The comparison came as no surprise to the architects, Italians Renzo Piano and Gianfranco Franchi, and Englishman Richard Rogers, who deliberately left the building's service systems visible. Some 11,000sq m (118,000sq ft) of glass, 15,000 tonnes of steel and 41 escalators make up a structure 42m high and 166m long (135 by 543ft).

The sloping **plaza** outside is one of Paris' most popular locations for street performers. Any time until 10pm you can take the free **escalators** that run in transparent tubes from the bottom left to the top right-hand corner and see Paris unfold before your eyes.

PLACE VENDOME

Louis XIV wanted the perfect setting for a monument to himself. He found it in the then Hôtel Vendôme, and in 1699 a statue of the king on horseback was erected in the centre of the square. As for the houses, only Louis' financiers could afford the rents. Now, the Ministry of Justice shares the square with banks, famous jewellers and

the Ritz Hotel. Like all royal statues, that of Louis XIV was overthrown during the Revolution. Its replacement, the Vendôme column, is a spiral of bronze reliefs commemorating the victories of Napoleon, cast from 1,250 cannon captured from the Austrians at Austerlitz and topped by a statue of the Emperor.

The modern complex of Forum des Halles contrasts with the late Gothic church of Saint-Eustache.

OPERA-GARNIER AND THE GRANDS BOULEVARDS

Window-shop your way past the goldsmiths and furriers of the Rue de la Paix to the ornate opera house (now sporting the name of its architect Charles Garnier to distinguish it from the new Opéra-Bastille, see p.49). Begun at the height of Napoleon III's Second Empire when Paris was Europe's most glamorous capital, it was only completed in 1875, after the Commune. The public rooms and the staircase are in the grand manner – more so even than the auditorium, which holds a mere 2,000 spectators. Underneath the building is a small lake, which provided the inspiration for the phantom's hiding place in Paul Leroux's *Phantom of the Opera*. The vast false ceiling was painted by Chagall in 1964. Now the home of the national ballet company, Opéra-Garnier was renovated in 1995.

A stock exchange, the Bank of France, a theatre: these were among the uses proposed for the huge neo-Classical church, **La Madeleine**. Napoleon's instinct was to turn it into a temple of glory for his army, but his architect suggested the Arc de Triomphe instead. The restored monarchy opted for a church, as originally intended when building started under Louis XV, and it was finally consecrated in 1842. Climb the steps for a great view down the Rue Royale to the Place de la Concorde and National Assembly beyond.

The **grands boulevards** which run from the Madeleine, past the Opéra and all the way to Place de la Bastille were the fashionable heart of Paris from the 1860s until well into the 20th century. They have fallen somewhat out of favour since, but their majestic sweep can still evoke former glories. On the Boulevard des Capucines, you can retrace the footsteps of Renoir, Manet and Pissarro as they took their paintings to Nadar's house, at no. 35, for the historic 1874 exhibition of Impressionism. Nowadays, the boulevards are the venue of a number of popular cinemas –

The pediment of the church of La Madeleine illustrates the story of Christ and Mary Magdalene.

appropriately enough, for it was at the Hôtel Scribe, near the Opéra, that the Lumière brothers staged the first public moving picture show in 1895.

 MONTMARTRE

Montmartre is the hilltop village, with its narrow, winding streets and dead-ends, which for the last 200 years has been associated with artists. The *Montmartrobus* spares you the walk and shows you some of the area in a single tour, but the best way to discover it at your own pace is to start early, and start at the top. Take the métro to Abbesses, use the elevator to the exit (the line runs deep below ground here) and notice the 1900 art nouveau entrance, saved from another station. Rue Yvonne le Tac leads to the base station of a funicular railway. It was here

that St Denis was martyred (see p.10, History) and where St Ignatius Loyola founded the Jesuit movement in 1534.

The funicular (it takes métro and bus tickets) climbs to the terrace in front of the Byzantine-style basilica of **Sacré-Cœur**. Standing at the highest point in Paris, it's one of the city's principal landmarks, and was for years one of the most controversial. Artists scorned it as a vulgar pastiche, and the working-class inhabitants of the area resented the way it was erected as a symbol of penitence for the insurrection of the 1871 Commune – they didn't feel penitent in the least. **43**

There has always been fierce argument over Sacré-Cœur, but no debate about the view.

The Sacré-Cœur's conspicuous whiteness comes from the local Château-Landon limestone, which bleaches on contact with carbon dioxide in the air and hardens with age. For many, the most striking feature of the basilica is the view of the city from the dome or the terrace below.

Just a few steps to the west of Sacré-Cœur, **Saint-Pierre-de-Montmartre** is one of the city's oldest churches. Consecrated in 1147, 16 years before the church of Saint-Germain-des-Prés (see p.57), it is a significant work of early Gothic, belied by its 18th-century façade. The Sacré-Cœur's architect, Paul Abadie, wanted to demolish Saint-Pierre, but he was overruled, and it was restored 'as a riposte to the Sacré-Cœur'.

The nearby **Place du Tertre** was once the centre of village life, where marriages were announced, militia men enlisted and criminals hanged. Try to visit during the early morning – before the mass-production 'artists' set up their easels and the crowds take over.

Just downhill in Place Emile Goudeau, no. 13 was the site of the studio of the **Bateau-Lavoir** (so-called because it resembled the laundry boats that used to travel along the Seine), before it was destroyed by fire. Here, if anywhere, was the birth place of modern art: Picasso, Braque and Juan Gris developed Cubism; Modigliani painted in a style all of his own, and Apollinaire wrote his first surrealistic verses. Some of their predecessors – Renoir, van Gogh and Gauguin – once lived and worked just north of Place du Tertre in Rue Cortot, Rue de l'Abreuvoir and Rue Saint-Rustique.

On the Rue Saint-Vincent at the corner of Rue des Saules, look out for Paris' last surviving **vineyard**, the tiny Clos de Montmartre. Then wind your way down Rue Lepic, a market street lined with marvellous food shops. Suddenly, at Place Blanche, everything changes. You hit Boulevard Clichy, or it hits you. Right on the corner is the Moulin Rouge, still staging its nightly cabarets – mostly to package tours. All the way east to **Place Pigalle** and beyond runs a ribbon of tawdry night-life with countless sex shops, peep shows and other dubious attractions, punctuated by a few conventional restaurants and bars. By evening, tour buses from all over Europe are parked nose to tail in the street. Later on, it's worth avoiding the métro here unless you want to share it with reeling drunks.

The principal **cemetery** of Montmartre, where luminaries of the arts such as the composers Berlioz and Offenbach lie buried, may seem a world away, but it's only a short walk from here to the entrance (west past the Moulin Rouge, then right at Avenue Rachel, see p.48, **Cemeteries**).

Portraits by numbers – they churn them out to order in Place du Tertre, Montmartre's square.

THE MARAIS

The district to the north of Ile de la Cité and Ile Saint-Louis has bravely withstood the onslaught of modern construction. It provides a remarkably authentic record of the development of the city, from the reign of Henri IV at the end of the 16th century to the advent of the Revolution. Built on reclaimed marshland as its name suggests, it contains some of Europe's most elegant Renaissance mansions (*hôtels*), many of which now serve as museums and libraries. The Marais has recently become fashionable again and trendy boutiques seem to spring up daily.

Take the métro to Rambuteau and start at the corner of the Rue des Archives and Rue des Francs-Bourgeois, named after the poor (not *bourgeois* at all) allowed to live here tax-free in the 14th century. The national archives are stored in an 18th-century mansion, the **Hôtel de Soubise**. Across a vast, horseshoe-shaped courtyard, you come across the exquisite Rococo style of Louis XV's time, in the apartments of the Prince and Princess of Soubise. Up on the first floor is the **Musée de l'Histoire de France**, with gems such as the only known portrait of Joan of Arc painted in her lifetime and the diary kept by Louis XVI.

Sun or shade? The arcades of the Place des Vosges have sheltered Parisians for centuries.

His entry for 14 July 1789, the day the Bastille was stormed, reads: *Rien* (nothing).

A garden (not always open to the public) connects the Hôtel de Soubise with its twin, the **Hôtel de Rohan**, on the Rue Vieille du Temple. Look out for Robert le Lorrain's fine *Les Chevaux d'Apollon*, over the old stables in the second courtyard, widely considered to be the most beautiful 18th-century sculpture in France.

Also on the Rue des Francs-Bourgeois, the Hôtel Carnavalet was the home of the lady of letters, Madame de Sévigné. Now it houses the **Musée Carnavalet** (see p.89).

The **Musée Picasso**, nearby at 5 Rue Thorigny, is housed in the beautifully restored Hôtel Salé (see p.85).

The Rue des Francs-Bourgeois ends at the loveliest residential square in Paris, **Place des Vosges**. Henri IV had it laid out in 1605 on the site of an old horse-market, his idea (borrowed from Catherine de Médici) being to have 'all the houses in the same symmetry'. After the wedding festivities of his son Louis XIII were held there, the gardens became the fashionable place to promenade, and later a spot for aristocratic duels. Today there's a children's playground, and the rest is perfect for just sitting.

The best time to see the square is in the winter, when the chestnut trees are bare and don't obscure the pink brick and honey-coloured stone façades. Victor Hugo, author of *Les Misérables*, lived at no. 6, now a museum housing many of his manuscripts, artefacts and wonderful drawings.

While in the Marais, take a wander round the old **Jewish quarter** (or *shtetl*, as the Paris Jews call it), especially if you are looking for somewhere unusual to eat. Jews have lived around the **Rue des Rosiers** for centuries, and the Rue Ferdinand Duval was known until 1900 as the Rue des Juifs. The other main street, Rue des Ecouffes (medieval slang for moneylenders), completes the lively shopping area, with delicatessens, kosher butchers and even kosher pizza shops. More recent arrivals from the Jewish **47**

Cemeteries

It's curiously calming to wander among the many tall tombs, packed together like rows of stone beach huts. Paris cemeteries are used to visitors and give out free maps so that you can go in search of the graves of the great.

Cimetière du Père Lachaise, north-east of Place de la Bastille, has seen an estimated 1,350,000 burials since its foundation in 1804. It even served as a battleground in 1871, when the Communards made a last stand. The Mur des Fédérés in the southeast corner marks the place where many were executed by firing squad. Celebrity tombs include those of the painter Ingres, dancer Isadora Duncan, composers Rossini and Chopin who made Paris their home, writers such as La Fontaine, Molière, Balzac, Proust, Oscar Wilde, his tomb marked by a fine monument by Jacob Epstein. More recent arrivals are Yves Montand, Simone Signoret and Jim Morrison of The Doors, who died mysteriously in Paris in 1971.

The tranquil **Cimetière de Montmartre**, below the hill, has an equally illustrious roll-call: Berlioz (buried with Harriet Smithson who inspired his *Symphonie Fantastique*), Offenbach, Degas, Feydeau, Nijinsky, the great chef Carême, film-maker François Truffaut, and Louise Weber, credited with inventing the cancan.

In the **Montparnasse** cemetery, you can find the tombs of composers Saint-Saëns and César Franck, writer Maupassant and poet Baudelaire, Dreyfus the Jewish officer whose conviction for spying split the nation, André Citroën the car maker, Pierre Laval the collaborationist Vichy prime minister (executed while dying from a suicide attempt), and philosopher Jean-Paul Sartre, who spent much of his later life on the Left Bank.

Beneath Montparnasse, the subterranean **Catacombs** are old quarries whose corridors were used in the past for the reburial of millions of skeletons removed from overcrowded cemeteries and charnel houses. Unidentified, they are stacked on shelves, piled in heaps or artfully arranged into macabre patterns. It's cold, damp and morbid, but if skulls and bones appeal, you'll find the main entrance in Place Denfert-Rochereau (shortened to Denfert, it sounds **48** just like the old name, *Place d'Enfer*, Hell Square).

communities of North Africa have replaced the Ashkenazim of Eastern Europe, who themselves took the place of the Sephardim who first settled in Paris in the 13th century.

BASTILLE

The large, circular **Place de la Bastille** is enjoying a new lease of life, taking over from Les Halles as a magnet for the in-crowd. No trace remains of the prison stormed in 1789: even the column in the centre commemorates a later revolution, that of 1830. Long a rundown area, it was given a shot in the arm by the construction of the **Opéra-Bastille**, one of former President Mitterand's great projects. This opened in 1990 to a chorus of hostile comment. Modernists attacked Carlos Ott's building as being too timid, conservatives said it was an ugly misfit, and you could say both camps had a point. Inside, the stark décor had its critics too, and rows about cost overruns and artistic policy led to resignations and firings even before the

opening. At least the acoustics were rated a success and soon the new home of the National Opera became part of the cultural life of Paris. Take a tour and try to go to a performance. In the adjacent streets, traditional old shops alternate with art galleries, artists' studios and restaurants, as in Rue de la Couronne. Just to the northeast of the Opéra in Rue de la Main d'Or, Rue de Lappe and their offshoots, clubs and discos have revived an old nightlife tradition.

Side by side in the Père Lachaise cemetery, the tombs of La Fontaine and Molière. **49**

Left Bank

The Left Bank (*rive gauche*) does its best to live up to a bohemian and intellectual image gained centuries ago. There is much more to it than the student life of the Latin Quarter, but so many schools and colleges are packed into a small area that it's the young who set the pace. Along nearby Boulevard Saint-Germain, writers and artists used to meet in the cafés of Saint-Germain-des-Prés: today's equivalent are the media people, film directors and journalists who still do. Montparnasse took over from Montmartre as the haunt of the avant-garde in the 1920s and still stakes a claim. The Left Bank has monuments and museums too, and many rate the Luxembourg Gardens as their favourite park. This side of the Seine too, you'll find markets and clusters of restaurants.

LATIN QUARTER

Just across the bridge from Notre-Dame is the point where the Latin Quarter begins. Here, the spirit of inquiry has traditionally been nurtured, sometimes leading to protest and outright revolt before subsiding into lifelong scepticism, as the rebels graduate from the university and move west to the more genteel *faubourg* of Saint-Germain. As far back as the 13th century, when Paris' first 'university' moved from the cloisters of Notre-Dame to

*L*ife on the Left Bank with a difference – houseboats floating on the Seine.

50

the Left Bank, the young came to the *quartier* – originally to learn Latin.

In those days the university simply meant a collection of scholars who met on a street corner, in a public square or courtyard to listen to a lecture given from a bench or balcony. Now open-air discussions may be held over coffee on some café terrace on the Boulevard Saint-Michel, or in the streets around the faculty buildings. Among the institutes of learning located here are the two most famous lycées, Henri IV

and Louis le Grand, where a large number of France's future élite are taught.

Begin your visit to the Latin Quarter at the **Place Saint-Michel**, where students still come to buy their books and stationery, or to gather round the bombastic 1860s fountain by Davioud, one of the great Paris meeting places. Plunge into the narrow streets of the **Saint-Séverin** quarter to the east (Rue Saint-Séverin, Rue de la Harpe and Rue Galande). You will discover a medieval world updated by the varied

exotica of smoky Greek barbecues, Tunisian pastry shops and a host of other eating establishments. One of the oldest churches in Paris, dating from between 1165 and 1220, little **Saint-Julien-le-Pauvre**, is a jewel of early Gothic architecture and now hosts chamber and religious music concerts. In an area packed with Middle Eastern restaurants, it's not unusual with its wafting incense and its mass said in Greek or Arabic (the church belongs to the Melchite sect of the Greek Orthodox Church). Just across Rue Saint-Jacques stands the exquisite 13th- to 15th-century Flamboyant Gothic **church of Saint-Séverin**, in which Dante is said to have prayed and Saint-Saëns asked to be honorary organist.

The Sorbonne

Named after the 13th-century college for theological students established by Robert de Sorbon, the university was later taken in hand by Cardinal Richelieu, who financed its reconstruction (1624-42). Few of the rather forbidding buildings are open to the public, but you can go inside the 17th-century **courtyard** with its ornate sundial and see the outside of the Baroque library and domed church. As you mingle with the students here, try to imagine the scene of May 1968. Protest against overcrowding, antiquated teaching, bureaucracy and the very basis of the social system made the Sorbonne a focal point for unrest in a year of ferment throughout Europe. When the police invaded the sanctuary – which for centuries had guaranteed student immunity – the revolt exploded onto the streets. Students and workers made common cause and there followed widespread national strikes which threatened the survival of the government. Over in the quiet, tree-shaded **Place de la Sorbonne**, it all seems a long time ago. One sad result was that in the aftermath, the Sorbonne was absorbed into the huge Paris Universities monolith and lost its independence.

Standing virtually opposite the Sorbonne's Rue des Ecoles

entrance, at 6 Place Paul-Painlevé, are the massive brick ruins of the ancient Roman public baths. They survived as part of an abbey – now the **Musée National du Moyen Age**, still often called by its former name, Musée de Cluny (see p.86). Its most famous exhibits are the wonderful 15th-century **tapestries**, the *Lady with the Unicorn*.

Pantheon

A stroll up the Rue Saint-Jacques past the most famous high school in Paris, the Lycée Louis le Grand, will bring you to the gigantic neo-Classical **Panthéon**. Designed for Louis XV as the church of Sainte-Geneviève (1755), it was secularized during the Revolution to serve as a mausoleum. But the Revolutionaries had a hard time deciding who deserved the honour. They agreed on Voltaire and Rousseau, but Mirabeau and Marat, admitted at first, were later expelled. In a deal with the Pope, Napoleon allowed church services to be held again. For most of

*T*he Left Bank's little church of Saint-Séverin is celebrated for its stonework and stained glass.

the 19th century the Panthéon oscillated between secular and consecrated status, according to the current régime's political colour. Finally Victor Hugo's funeral in 1885 settled the issue in favour of a secular mausoleum. He was followed by realist writer, Emile Zola, **53** socialist leader Jean Jaurès, Léon Gambetta (leader during the 1870 siege of Paris), Louis Braille (inventor of the blind alphabet), Pierre and Marie Curie (discoverers of radium) and many others.

The sight of the massive portico (bearing the inscription 'To great men, the Motherland's gratitude') is impressive, but the empty interior is

Bakers start work long before dawn, producing works of art that appeal to all the senses.

sterile, its windows covered by huge, late 19th-century paintings depicting the stories of St Denis, St Geneviève, Clovis and Joan of Arc. The crypt is even more dispiriting, a grim maze of corridors lined with cells containing the tombs of the famous, as well as many which few will have heard of. A good display on the history of the Panthéon is the best part of the visit.

Escape to the old streets behind the Panthéon, where the bustling **Rue Mouffetard** and its offshoots are more like a village than part of Paris. The stalls of the morning market (see p.100) are piled with superb produce and half fill the street. Here and in the tiny Place de la Contrescarpe you will find one of the largest choices of ethnic restaurants in the city, especially Thai, Vietnamese and Chinese.

A block to the east is where signs to **Arènes de Lutèce** lead you to a little park. Enter, and you will find the Roman amphitheatre, restored after its remains were found during the 19th century.

JARDIN DU LUXEMBOURG

Bright with flowers, scattered with statues of famous characters, the Luxembourg Gardens are the prettiest green space on the Left Bank. Students find quiet corners to read or relax; children can sail their boats on the octagonal pond or ride a merry-go-round designed by none other than Charles Garnier, architect of the Opéra (see p.42) and old men meet under the chestnut trees to play chess or a game of *boules*.

The Palais du Luxembourg, built for Marie de Médici early in the 17th century, now houses the French Senate.

EAST ALONG THE SEINE

Back down by the Seine, but heading eastwards, stroll past the Jussieu University complex that stands on the site of the Halles aux Vins (wine market). The **Institut du Monde Arabe** (Arab World Institute) is at 23 Quai Saint-Bernard (open 1-8pm, closed Sundays and Mondays), and was built with the help of 16 Arab nations to foster cultural links between the Islamic world and the West. A modern glass box of a building, it recalls Islamic tradition in the geometric patterns of its south-facing façade. The fine museum inside traces the cultures of the Arab world, both the pre-Islamic and Islamic periods, with superb exhibits, well displayed. The best way to see them is to start on the 7th floor and work down. A library of over 40,000 volumes covers all aspects of Arab culture. The rooftop restaurant's menu includes every Middle Eastern dish you could think of.

The **Jardin des Plantes** next door, created by Louis XIII as 'a royal garden of medicinal plants' is still an excellent botanical and decorative garden, with exotic plants in the hothouses. The adjoining **Musée d'Histoire Naturelle**, with armies of skeletons, butterflies and mineral samples, is resolutely old-fashioned.

The vast grey **Ministère de l'Economie et des Finances** with one foot in the water on **55** the other side of the Seine is part of the conspicuous redevelopment of the Bercy district, including a new bridge, Pont Charles de Gaulle.

SAINT-GERMAIN-DES-PRES

This Left Bank area is one of the most attractive neighbourhoods in all Paris. Not part of the Latin Quarter, but rather an extension of it, this is the home of numerous publishing houses, the Académie Française, expensive interior design and fashion shops, bookshops to suit all tastes and café terraces designed for people-watching. It used to be the headquarters of Jean-Paul Sartre and his existentialist acolytes who would wear, winter or summer, black corduroys and long woollen scarves. In Place Saint-Germain-des-Prés, the Café Bonaparte on the north side and the Deux Magots on the west provide ring-side seats for a street theatre of mimes, musicians and neighbourhood eccentrics.

The Café de Flore round the corner has hung on to its intellectual tradition more than the others, perhaps because of its rather ideologically confused history. It has been home successively to the extreme right Action Française group under Charles Maurras in 1899, the poet and surrealist precursor Apollinaire in 1914 (who, with his friends, liked to provoke brawls), and then Sartre's existentialists during the 1950s, a peaceful bunch who never got enough sleep to have the energy to fight.

Also on the Place Saint-Germain stands the **church of Saint-Germain-des-Prés**, the oldest in Paris. It is a mixture of Romanesque and Gothic, with a clock-tower dating from about the year 1000 and a 17th-century porch sheltering 12th-century doorposts. The interior was restored after the Revolutionaries gutted it and

The Luxembourg Gardens are the Left Bank's loveliest park. The Senate meets in the Palace.

used it as a gunpowder factory. It makes a wonderful venue for frequent concerts.

To the north of the square the Rue Bonaparte leads the way past the **Ecole Nationale Supérieure des Beaux-Arts** (Fine Arts School). This structure incorporates fragments of medieval and Renaissance architecture and sculpture that make it a living museum. During the events of May 1968, it became something of a poster factory for the overnight creations of the students.

The very august **Palais de l'Institut de France**, home of the Académie Française, is on the Quai de Conti by the Pont des Arts. Designed by Louis le Vau in 1668 to harmonize with the Louvre across the river, the Institut began as a school for the sons of provincial gentry, financed by a legacy of Cardinal Mazarin. Then, in 1805 the building was turned over to the Institut, which comprises the Académie Française – the supreme arbiter of the French language founded by Cardinal Richelieu in 1635 – and the Académies des Belles-Lettres, **57**

Sciences, Beaux-Arts and Sciences Morales et Politiques. The admission of a new member to the Académie Française is the occasion of great ceremony. Guides to the Institut like to point out the east pavilion, site of the old 14th-century Tour de Nesle. They say that Queen Jeanne de Bourgogne used the tower to watch out for likely young lovers, whom she summoned for the night and then had thrown into the Seine.

MONTPARNASSE

Don't go looking for a hill: the Mount Parnassus in its name was a mound left after quarrying, and has long since been removed. This is the quarter where they invented the cancan in 1845, at the Grande Chaumière dancehall (now defunct). In the twenties, it took over from Montmartre as the stamping ground of the city's artistic colony, or at least its avant-garde, as Picasso moved over. Expatriates such as Hemingway, Gertrude Stein, F. Scott Fitzgerald and John dos Passos also took to the free-living atmosphere and added to the mystique themselves. The attraction isn't immediately evident: the wide, straight **Boulevard du Montparnasse** is plain by Paris standards. Nowadays, the majority of the haunts where the Lost Generation found itself have been polished and painted, or even entirely rebuilt, but plenty of people think it worth paying the elevated prices to feel they might be sitting in a seat once warmed by Modigliani, Lenin or Sartre.

The tall (59-storey), black **Tour Montparnasse** may be an egregious eyesore, but the view from the top is marvellous (33 Avenue du Maine, open daily 9.30am-10pm). The adjoining Centre Commercial has some good shopping and it's also well worth taking a look at the modern Gare Montparnasse nearby.

The **cemetery** (see p.48) to the east of the station, reached from Boulevard Edgar Quinet, is the resting place of some famous and controversial figures in French history.

Cafés with a past

Many of the cafés once frequented by great artists and thinkers still flourish – although today's prices might come as a shock.

St Germain-des-Prés. Camus, Sartre and Simone de Beauvoir used to meet at *Les Deux Magots* at 170 Blvd St-Germain, 75006. Now it's something of a tourist show in the summer (closed August). Another favourite was *Café de Flore*, right next door (closed July). *Le Procope*, 13 Rue de l'Ancienne Comédie, 75006, was the first coffee-house in Paris, dating from 1686; it's said that Voltaire drank 40 cups a day here, and that the young Napoleon had to leave his hat as security while he went for money to pay the bill; now it's just a restaurant, with good value, fixed price menus.

Montparnasse. One of Henry Miller's hang-outs, *Le Select* (99 Blvd. du Montparnasse, 75006) opened as an all-night bar in 1925; les Six, the group of composers including Erik Satie and Francis Poulenc met here. *La Coupole* opposite (102 Blvd. du Montparnasse, 75014) was a favourite with Sartre and de Beauvoir in the years after World War II; it has been rebuilt and now seats 400. *Le Dôme* at no. 108 has lost some of its character since the days of Modigliani and Stravinsky, with elaborate remodelling. Across the street, Picasso, Derain and Vlaminck used to meet at the *Rotonde* (105 Blvd. du Montparnasse, 75006). At the junction of Boulevard du Montparnasse and Boulevard Saint-Michel, *La Closerie des Lilas* is where Lenin and Trotsky plotted before the Russian Revolution, and where Hemingway and his buddies met after World War I.

Right Bank. The resplendent *Café de la Paix* in Le Grand Hôtel at 12 Blvd des Capucins, 75009 (see p.77) was a favourite with the Prince of Wales (later Edward VII) and Oscar Wilde, Zola and Maupassant; Caruso also used to dine here after singing at the Opéra across the street. Near Les Halles, *La Promenade de Vénus* at 44 Rue du Louvre, 75001 was the 1920's headquarters of André Breton and his fellow surrealists. Market workers and celebrities used to share the 24-hour *Au Pied de Cochon* (At the Pig's Foot), 6 Rue Coquillière, 75001 (see p.77). In the Marais, Lenin and Trotsky (again) met at *La Tartine*, 24 Rue de Rivoli, 75004, a dark little local bar at the unfashionable end of this long street. **59**

INVALIDES

Geographically if not temperamentally part of the Left Bank, the Palais-Bourbon is the seat of the **Assemblée Nationale** (parliament). It makes a stately riverside façade for the 7th district, with its 18th-century embassies, ministries and private mansions (*hôtels particuliers*). Napoleon added the Grecian columns facing the Pont de la Concorde: the more graceful character of the Palais-Bourbon is seen from its entrance on the south side. Designed for a daughter of Louis XIV in 1722, it can be entered only on written request or as the guest of a deputy. If you do get in, look for the Delacroix paintings in the library, illustrating the history of civilization.

The Prime Minister's splendid residence, at 57 Rue de Varenne, is a short walk from the National Assembly. Its private park has a music pavilion favoured for secret strategy sessions. The same quiet 18th-century street holds the **Rodin Museum** at no 77, in the delightful Hôtel Biron (see p.89),

where some of the great sculptor's most famous works are on display.

The most important sight in the area, however, is the monumentally impressive **Hôtel des Invalides**, which was established by Louis XIV as the first national hospital and retirement home for soldiers wounded during action. At one time it housed approximately 6,000 veterans, but Napoleon took over part of it to form the **Musée de l'Armée** (army museum), which still occupies a large proportion. Then the Invalides came to symbolize the glory of Napoleon himself, when his remains were finally brought back from St Helena in 1840 for burial in the chapel under the golden **Dôme**. His massive tomb of red porphyry rests on a pedestal of green granite from the Vosges. His brother Joseph, installed for a while on the throne of Spain, has his monument in the upper gallery, and his son, given the title of King of Rome when a baby, is buried in the crypt.

The main courtyard allows access to the adjoining church

of **Saint-Louis-des-Invalides**, decorated with flags taken by French armies in battle since Waterloo. The courtyard itself contains the 18 cannon, including eight taken from Vienna, which Napoleon ordered to be fired on great occasions – such as the birth of his son in 1811. The cannon sounded again for the 1918 Armistice and the funeral of Marshal Foch in 1929.

Just on the southwest corner of the Invalides is the **Ecole Militaire** where officers have trained since the middle of the 18th century. Their former parade ground, the vast **Champ de Mars**, is now a green park stretching all the way to the Eiffel Tower. Horse races were held here in the 1780s, and also five World Fairs between 1867 and 1937. In the 20th century it has become the front lawn of the Left Bank's most luxurious residences.

EIFFEL TOWER

Right from the start, it was a resounding success. In 1889, 2 million visitors paid 5 francs a head to climb to the top, and the figures have shown consistently that, whatever its critics may have said, the Tower has its place in Paris' landscape.

Some monuments celebrate heroes, commemorate victories, honour kings or saints. This is a monument for its own sake. Its construction for the

*R*odin's The Thinker, *in the* garden of the Rodin Museum, *with the Dôme of Les Invalides.*

World Fair of 1889 was an astounding engineering achievement – some 15,000 pieces of metal joined by 2,500,000 rivets, soaring 320m (984ft) into the sky on a base only 130m (430ft) across.

At the time, it was the tallest structure in the world. It also provided the perfect perch for transmitters when radio and TV came along.

On its inauguration, the lifts were not yet in operation and Prime Minister Tirard stopped at the first platform (57m or 187ft up), leaving his Minister of Commerce to go all the way to the top to present Gustave Eiffel with the Legion of Honour medal. Conceived purely as a temporary structure for the Fair, the tower was slated for destruction in 1910, but nobody had the heart to take it down. When new spotlights were installed in 1985 to illuminate the tower from within, even detractors had to admit that it did have something.

An audio-visual show about the tower is screened on the first platform; there are restaurants on the first and second, and a bar on the third. On a pollution-free day, you can see for approximately 65km (40 miles) from the top, but more often the view is clearer from the second platform. Try to get there an hour before sunset for the best light.

*P*leasure boats and working barges alike tie up at the Port de Suffren, near the Eiffel Tower.

Western Outskirts

Bois de Boulogne

The chic 16th *arrondissement* is bordered on its west side by the capital's biggest park, 900 hectares (2,200 acres) of green space, lakes and woodland. The remnant of an old hunting forest, it was tamed by Baron Haussmann into resembling a London park. The **Bagatelle**, once a royal retreat, has a very lovely English garden, bursting with flowers during spring and early summer. The **Jardin d'Acclimatation** is an amusement park with plenty of attractions for children: shows, rides and a small zoo. There are bikes for rent outside its entrance for exploring the rest of the Bois. The **Musée des Arts et Traditions Populaires** has excellent displays of folk art and craft through the ages. Also within the park are a boating lake and two fine racecourses, Longchamp for flat races and Auteuil for steeplechases. *Warning*: in spite of police patrols, after dark parts of the Bois de Boulogne are reckoned to be the most dangerous place in Paris.

La Défense

At the end of the long Avenue de la Grande-Armée leaving from l'Etoile, the battery of towers grows bigger and bigger as you approach through the elegant, leafy suburb of Neuilly. Cross the river and there you are: in a mini-Manhattan that has grown by fits and starts since 1969 to become a city in its own right. In the process, it has somehow managed to get a soul, in spite of the inhuman scale of some of its windswept spaces.

The Grande Arche is further away than most of the towers, and only when you get close do you realize just how big it is. A hollow cube 110m high and 106m wide (360 by 347ft), it's broad enough to straddle the Champs-Elysées and high enough for Notre-Dame to fit underneath. Built with remarkable speed (Danish architect Johann-Otto von Sprekelsen **63**

*T*he Grande Arche de la Défense could straddle the full width of the Champs-Elysées.

won the contest in 1983 and it was ready for the bicentenary of the French Revolution in 1989), the Grande Arche lies directly in line with the Arc de Triomphe and the Cour Carrée of the Louvre. Its white gables are clothed in Carrara marble, the outer façades with a combination of grey marble and glass; the inside walls are covered with aluminium.

The two 'legs' contain offices, while the roof houses conference rooms and exhibition space. Bubble lifts whisk you up through a fibreglass and Teflon 'cloud', held by steel cables that stretch from one wall to the other, but unless you have a museum pass, the ride to the top is expensive and the view not much more striking than from the terrace.

The curious visiting crowds as well as the thousands who work here have encouraged the opening of more and more shops, cinemas, hotels and restaurants. One of the cinemas, near the Grande Arche, has a big wraparound IMAX screen, and in the same building the **Musée de l'Automobile** displays over 100 classic cars, restored to mint condition.

Across the main concourse a 12m (39ft) bronze thumb by César sticks out like, well, a sore thumb. Stroll down the tiers of terraces and you'll find many more statues, fountains and murals by Miró, Calder and other modern artists, all detailed on street-plans given out at information desks.

A Selection of Hotels and Restaurants

Recommended Hotels

The list is divided geographically into: Right Bank – central and west (1-2, 8-9, 16-18); Right Bank – east and Ile Saint-Louis (3-4, 10-11, 19-20); Left Bank (5-7, 14-15). The numbers indicate the *arrondissement* (district), also given by the last one or two figures in the postal code, e.g. 75015 is the 15th.

The following ranges give an idea of the price for a double room, per night, with private bath unless otherwise stated. Service and tax are included, but not breakfast. Note that prices can vary widely within a hotel, and may change according to the time of year. Always confirm the price when booking.

🏨🏨🏨🏨🏨	over 2200F
🏨🏨🏨🏨	1500-2200F
🏨🏨🏨	900-1500F
🏨🏨	450-900F
🏨	below 450F

RIGHT BANK – CENTRAL AND WEST (1-2, 8-9, 16-18)

Baltimore 🏨🏨🏨🏨

88-bis Avenue Kléber, 75016
Tel. 44 34 54 54; fax 44 34 54 44
105 rooms. A modern hotel with a classic look, beautifully decorated rooms and friendly personal service. A few minutes' walk from l'Etoile and with Boissière métro station close at hand. The prize-winning Le Bertie's restaurant offers traditional English dishes with French flair (the menu is planned by Albert Roux).

Bradford Elysées 🏨🏨

10 Rue St-Philippe-du-Roule, 75008
Tel. 45 63 20 20; fax 45 63 20 07
48 rooms. A friendly hotel in a peaceful street between Rue du Faubourg-St-Honoré and Champs-Elysées, close to St-Philippe-du-Roule métro. A member of the Best Western reservation system.

Chopin 🏨🏨

46 Passage Jouffroy (at 10 Blvd Montmartre), 75009
Tel. 47 70 58 10; fax 42 47 00 70
36 rooms. Situated along one of the capital's traditional covered

passages (arcades) with antique shops as its neighbours, this is a very comfortable, old-established and beautifully renovated hotel. Close to Richelieu-Drouot métro station.

Claridge Bellman ▯▯▯
37 Rue François-Ier, 75008
Tel. 47 23 54 42; fax 47 23 08 84
42 rooms. A small hotel offering the personal touch, in the stylish district lying between the Seine and the Champs-Elysées, home of many of the great names in the fashion world. The rooms are delightfully furnished with antiques. No restaurant.

Concorde-St-Lazare ▯▯▯
108 Rue St-Lazare, 75008
Tel. 40 08 44 44; fax 42 93 01 20
300 rooms. A classic 19th-century building listed as a national monument, and very carefully restored. Within easy reach of the Opéra, the large department stores on Boulevard Haussmann, and St-Lazare station. The well-known Terminus restaurant is housed in the same building.

Hôtel de Crillon ▯▯▯▯▯
10 Place de la Concorde, 75008
Tel. 44 71 15 00; fax 44 71 15 02
163 rooms. The splendid classical façade of this world-famous hotel dominates the north side of Place de la Concorde. Renowned primarily for its impeccable service and quality, but also for the two notable restaurants, Les Ambassadeurs and the more affordable L'Obélisque.

Dorée ▯
66 Boulevard Barbès, 75018
Tel. 42 23 52 36; fax 42 54 22 55
55 rooms. A pleasant, older hotel at an economical price, situated on the edge of Montmartre just below Sacré-Cœur. On a busy street but well sound-proofed. Some rooms face a quiet garden.

Ducs d'Anjou ▯▯
1 Rue Sainte-Opportune, 75001
Tel. 42 36 92 24; fax 42 36 16 63
38 rooms. A well-renovated older building in the middle of the bustling Les Halles district, so rooms facing the street can be slightly noisy at night.

Duminy-Vendôme ▯▯
3 Rue du Mont-Thabor, 75001
Tel. 42 60 32 80; fax 42 96 07 83
77 rooms. Just a few steps from the pleasant Tuileries gardens, this is a comfortable establishment priding itself on its attractively decorated rooms: brass beds, flowery wallpaper and full-blown marble bathrooms.

67

Hôtel de l'Elysée

12, Rue des Saussaies, 75008
Tel. 42 65 29 25; fax 42 65 64 28
32 rooms. A small and rather elegant hotel, with good views and attractive décor, in a quiet street near the presidential Elysée Palace and the upmarket shopping in Rue du Faubourg-St-Honoré.

France et Choiseul

239 Rue St. Honoré, 75001
Tel. 42 61 54 60; fax 40 20 96 32
86 rooms. In a central situation, close to Place Vendôme, convenient for the fashionable shops. This is a traditional, rather old-fashioned hotel, with fine antique furniture, but the amenities are fully up to modern standards and service is polished.

Grand Hôtel Inter-Continental

2 Rue Scribe, 75009
Tel. 40 07 32 32; fax 42 66 12 51
514 rooms. Standing across from the Opéra-Garnier, taking up most of a triangular block, this historic hotel was opened by Empress Eugénie in 1862. It has been extensively renovated in recent years. The Café de la Paix, with its original gold and green décor restored, is a national monument. La Verrière garden restaurant occupies the lovely central courtyard.

Henri IV

25 Place Dauphine, 75001
Tel. 43 54 44 53; no fax
22 rooms. A modest budget hotel, one of the very limited number of places to stay on the Ile de la Cité. Somewhat old-fashioned rooms, with shared bathrooms. Only a short walk from Notre-Dame and Saint-Michel. You will need to reserve well in advance.

Lord Byron

5 Rue Chateaubriand, 75008
Tel. 43 59 89 98; fax 42 89 46 04
31 rooms. A pleasant small hotel, reasonably priced for its location just east of l'Etoile, with fair-sized rooms, stylish décor and an elegant courtyard.

Magellan

17 Rue J-B Dumas, 75017
Tel. 45 72 44 51; fax 40 68 90 36
75 rooms. Comfortable hotel in a quiet location, with an attractive garden and a sauna and exercise room. Well placed for Palais des Congrès convention centre.

Méridien Etoile

81 Blvd. Gouvion-St-Cyr, 75017
Tel. 40 68 34 34; fax 40 68 31 31
1025 rooms. Bright, modern and efficient, and close to the Bois de Boulogne, the Air France city terminal and the Palais des Congrès

convention centre. The hotel has its own executive floor, pleasant French and Japanese restaurants, and also the Lionel Hampton jazz club with frequent visiting soloists and groups.

New Montmartre   ▯▯
7 Rue Paul Albert, 75018
Tel. 46 06 03 03; fax 46 06 73 28
32 rooms. This is a pleasant and quite spacious budget hotel, on the eastern slopes of Montmartre just below Sacré-Cœur. Near Anvers métro station.

Regent's Garden   ▯▯
6 Rue Pierre-Demours, 75017
Tel. 45 74 07 30; fax 40 55 01 42
39 rooms. A friendly small hotel in a tranquil situation just north of l'Etoile, with an attractive garden and also a fitness room. A member of the Best Western reservation system.

Terrass' Hotel   ▯▯▯
12 Rue Joseph-de-Maistre, 75018
Tel. 46 06 72 85; fax 42 52 29 11
101 rooms. Long established as the leading hotel in Montmartre, set on the quiet western edge of the hill, with striking views over the capital. Indoor restaurant and piano bar, as well as La Terrasse roof-top restaurant open between May and September.

RIGHT BANK – EAST (3-4, 10-11, 19-20)

Bastille   ▯▯
14 Rue de la Roquette
Tel. 44 70 24 24; fax 44 70 24 51
30 rooms. A beautifully renovated and brightly decorated small hotel, in the heart of the revived Bastille district, next to art galleries, close to the Opéra-Bastille and nightlife.

Beaumarchais   ▯
3 Rue Oberkampf, 75011
Tel. 43 38 16 16; fax 43 38 32 86
33 rooms. A pleasant, modernized budget hotel. Not far from the little streets and markets of the temple quarter, and convenient for the Gare de Lyon.

Champagne Mulhouse   ▯▯
87 Blvd de Strasbourg, 75010
Tel. 42 09 12 28; fax 42 09 48 12
31 rooms, some with balconies and some facing a quiet courtyard. A modest hotel, simply but well furnished, and recently renovated. Opposite Gare de l'Est, close by Gare du Nord and near to a profusion of restaurants.

Crimée   ▯
188 Rue de Crimée, 75019
Tel. 40 36 75 29; fax 40 36 29 57
31 rooms. Modern and comfortable. Away from the centre on the **69**

northeastern edge of the city, but good value and very convenient for La Villette (Cité des Sciences and Cité de la Musique). Close to métro station Crimée.

Des Deux-Iles

59 Rue St-Louis en-l'Ile, 75004
Tel. 43 26 13 35; fax 43 29 60 25
17 rooms. Set in a small and attractive 17th-century mansion on the main street of the tranquil Ile Saint-Louis, this hotel is comfortable and friendly, with a cellar bar. Rooms are compact but attractively decorated.

Grand Hôtel Jeanne d'Arc

3 Rue Jarente, 75004
Tel. 48 87 62 11; fax 48 87 37 31
36 rooms. An attractive small establishment in a calm location, on the edge of the Marais near Place des Vosges and the Jewish quarter. Popular with foreign visitors, and necessary to reserve in advance.

Jeu de Paume

54 Rue St-Louis-en-l'Ile, 75004
Tel. 43 26 14 18; fax 40 46 02 76
32 rooms. In a delightful situation on quiet Ile Saint-Louis. The hotel has kept its ancient, 17th-century 'jeu de paume' court: a game said to be the predecessor of tennis. Great for a taste of old Paris.

Le Laumière

4 Rue Petit, 75019
Tel. 42 06 10 77; fax 42 06 72 50
54 rooms. This is an excellent, value-for-money hotel, with modern, comfortable rooms, and deservedly popular. Some way from the centre, between Parc Butte-Chaumont and la Villette, close to Laumière métro station.

Lutèce

65 Rue St-Louis-en-l'Ile, 75004
Tel. 43 26 23 52; fax 43 29 60 25
23 rooms. A small and charming hotel on the quiet, select Ile Saint-Louis, with very attractive little rooms. Those on the 6th floor are the most romantic.

Mary's

15 Rue de Malte, 75011
Tel. 47 00 81 70; fax 47 00 58 06
38 rooms, most with private bathroom. A basic but clean and functional establishment at a budget price. Convenient for the Bastille area and its boutiques, galleries and varied nightlife.

Picard

26 Rue de Picardy, 75003
Tel. 48 87 53 82; fax 48 87 02 56
30 rooms. A small and friendly budget hotel. Only half the rooms have private bathrooms. Located in the Temple area of little streets

and old shops, looking out on the *Carreau du Temple*, site of a lively daily market.

Pyrenées-Gambetta

12 Rue Père Lachaise, 75020
Tel. 47 97 76 57; fax 47 97 17 61
32 rooms. An agreeable and quiet budget hotel on the north-eastern edge of the city, close to the Père Lachaise cemetery and Gambetta métro station. A small number of rooms at a lower price do not have private bathrooms.

Saint-Laurent Gare de l'Est

5 Rue Saint-Laurent, 75010
Tel. 42 09 59 79; fax 42 09 83 50
44 rooms. A simple, comfortable and clean hotel, especially convenient for the stations, Gare de l'Est and Gare du Nord. There is a large and varied choice of restaurants close at hand.

Terminus Nord

12 Blvd. de Denain, 75010
Tel. 42 80 20 00; fax 42 80 63 89
245 rooms. This 1865 railway station hotel is right opposite the Gare du Nord, perfectly situated for arrivals by Eurostar. It was beautifully restored in 1993, and the rooms are attractively decorated and well-equipped. The balconies of some upper storey rooms look across to Sacré Cœur. The 1925 Terminus restaurant is in the same building.

LEFT BANK (5-7, 14-15)

Abbaye Saint-Germain

10 Rue Cassette, 75006
Tel. 45 44 38 11; fax 45 48 07 86
46 rooms. A 17th-century abbey, situated between the Luxembourg Gardens and Saint-Germain-des-Prés, which has been beautifully adapted into a hotel. Some rooms have original wooden beams, but all modern comforts as well. The staff are helpful and attentive.

Alésia-Montparnasse

84 Rue Raymond Losserand, 75014
Tel. 45 42 16 03; fax 45 42 11 60
45 rooms. A good base in Montparnasse, with compact but well-furnished rooms. The location is handy for the restaurants and cafés and not far from the station.

Angleterre St-Germain

44 Rue Jacob, 75006
Tel. 42 60 34 72; fax 42 60 16 93
27 rooms. A charming hotel in a historic house, with a garden. A ceremonial staircase leads to elegant rooms. Ernest Hemingway lodged here in the 1920s.

71

Cayré IIII

4 Blvd Raspail, 75007
Tel. 45 44 38 88; fax 45 44 98 13
119 rooms. Known for its traditional good service and unusually large rooms. Set in the attractive quarter behind the Musée d'Orsay, the hotel has long been a favourite with artists and writers.

Duc de Saint-Simon IIII

14 Rue de Saint-Simon, 75007
Tel. 44 39 20 20; fax 45 48 68 25
34 rooms. At the very heart of the Faubourg Saint-Germain, near the Musée d'Orsay. This is an attractively furnished early 19th-century town house that seems to come straight out of a Balzac novel. Has a lovely private garden.

Elysées-Maubourg II

35 Blvd de la Tour-Maubourg, 75007
Tel. 45 56 10 78; fax 47 05 65 08
30 rooms. A small hotel with welcoming service and atmosphere, fine décor and comfortable rooms. On sunny days, the tiny interior courtyard is open and makes an attractive setting for afternoon tea.

Esmeralda I

4 Rue St-Julien-le-Pauvre, 75005
Tel. 43 54 19 20; fax 40 51 00 68
16 rooms. A modest budget hotel in an old house in a fascinating part of the Left Bank, looking across at Ile de la Cité and Notre Dame. Most rooms do not have a private bathroom.

Lutétia IIIII

45 Blvd Raspail, 75006
Tel. 49 54 46 46; fax 49 54 46 00
273 rooms. One of the few large old, traditional hotels on the Left Bank, friendly and welcoming. Its art deco architecture and interior design has been well preserved. The Brasserie Lutétia is popular with locals as well as visitors.

Hôtel des Marronniers II

21 Rue Jacob, 75006
Tel. 43 25 30 60; fax 40 46 83 56
37 rooms. A tall, narrow but most attractive hotel with its own small garden and chestnut trees (hence the hotel's name), just one block from the Place St-Germain-des-Prés with its famous cafés.

Nikko IIIII

61 Quai de Grenelle, 75015
Tel. 40 58 20 00; fax 45 75 42 35
779 rooms. A modern and well-equipped international hotel, with a swimming pool and sauna, and notable restaurants: Les Célébrités, Brasserie Pont Mirabeau and the Japanese Benkay. View over the Pont Mirabeau and the Seine, not far from the Eiffel Tower.

Palais Bourbon ▐▐

49 Rue de Bourgogne, 75007
Tel. 45 54 63 32; fax 45 55 20 21
32 rooms. Near the National Assembly and Rodin Museum, a fine old building with attractive, good-sized rooms. Reasonably priced for the location, it is very popular, so reserve well in advance.

Le Pavillon ▐▐

54 Rue Saint Dominique, 75007
Tel. 45 51 42 87; fax 45 51 32 79
18 rooms. An attractive little place on a quiet courtyard near Les Invalides. It is a former convent so the rooms are quite small.

Relais Medicis ▐▐▐

23 Rue Racine, 75006
Tel. 43 26 00 60; fax 40 46 83 39
16 rooms. A small and attractively decorated hotel, with oak-beamed rooms set around a quiet courtyard with a fountain, just off Boulevard Saint-Michel and close to the Luxembourg gardens.

Saint-André-des-Arts ▐

66 Rue Saint-André-des-Arts, 75006
Tel. 43 26 96 16; fax 43 29 73 34
33 rooms. A friendly small establishment with a lively atmosphere and a central position in the heart of the Latin Quarter. A few rooms do not have private bathrooms.

Saint Pères ▐▐▐

65 Rue des Saints-Pères, 75006
Tel. 45 44 50 00; fax 45 44 90 83
39 rooms. Quiet and comfortable, with modern bedrooms, this is a hotel favoured by the publishing world, who meet over breakfast in the small courtyard. Close to Place St-Germain-des-Prés and its famous café terraces.

Sèvres Vaneau ▐▐

86 Rue Vaneau, 75007
Tel. 45 48 73 11; fax 45 49 27 74
39 rooms. A friendly small hotel, recently restored and attractively redecorated. The area is quiet, yet not far from the Boulevard Saint-Germain, its cafés and bookshops.

Tour Eiffel-Duplus ▐▐

11 Rue Juge, 75015
Tel. 45 78 29 29; fax 45 78 60 00
40 rooms. A bright, newly converted hotel in a quiet street, with small but attractive rooms, some overlooking a garden courtyard. Breakfast buffet in garden room. Close to Dupleix métro station.

De Turenne ▐

20 Avenue de Tourville, 75007
Tél. 47 05 99 92; fax 45 56 06 04
34 rooms. A budget hotel with attractive décor and cosy rooms, offering good value for this part of the city, next to Les Invalides.

73

Recommended Restaurants

In this section the term restaurant includes bistros and brasseries (see p.108). The price ranges quoted are per person, for a three-course dinner with a glass or two of house wine, tax and service included. Extras will send bills much higher, but conversely, a modest lunch menu can cost much less.

▊▊▊▊	over 600F
▊▊▊	400-600F
▊▊	250-400F
▊	below 250F

RIGHT BANK – CENTRAL AND WEST (1-2, 8-10, 16-18)

Maison D'Alsace   ▊▊▊
39 Avenue des Champs-Elysées, 75008
Tel. 43 59 44 24
A big, classic brasserie, on the Champs-Elysées, open 24 hours a day, every day, for Alsace specialities and excellent seafood. Offers budget menus after 11pm.

L'Appart   ▊▊
9 Rue du Colisée, 75008
Tel. 53 75 16 34
Close to the Champs-Elysées, a modern bistro that looks more like someone's apartment (hence the name). The cooking is creative but not fussy: colourful salads, pan-fried fish and calf's liver, reasonably priced wines. Closed Sunday.

Beauvilliers   ▊▊▊
52 Rue Lamarck, 75018
Tel. 42 54 54 42
A restaurant in the unusual setting of an old bakery and bread shop, with a terrace for outdoor dining. The menu concentrates on classic cuisine. Closed Monday at lunchtime, Sunday and public holidays.

Le Canard d'Avril   ▊
5 Rue Paul Lelong, 75002
Tel. 42 36 26 08
A casual and colourful bistro featuring delicious dishes from southwestern France – especially duck (as the name implies). Closed Saturday and Sunday.

Carré des Feuillants   ▊▊▊▊
14 Rue de Castiglione, 75001
Tel. 42 86 82 82
Alain Dutournier is one of the most acclaimed chefs in Paris and

you need to reserve days ahead. His cuisine has a distinct flavour of the southwest (Armagnac). The setting is an old convent, with futuristic décor. Closed Saturday lunch-time, Sunday and August.

Charlot Roi des Coquillages

12 Place de Clichy, 75009
Tel. 48 74 49 64

Fish and shellfish, as fresh as can be, are simply and skilfully prepared. One of the best places in Paris to try a bouillabaisse in the true Marseilles style. Open every day; last orders 1am.

Chartier

7 Rue du Faubourg Montmartre, 75009
Tel. 47 70 86 29

This is the place for one of the least expensive meals in town, attracting noisy, happy hordes on account of its low prices and good, traditional French cooking. With loads of character and atmosphere. Open until 9pm.

Chez Pauline

5 Rue Villedon, 75001
Tel. 42 96 20 70

An old-established bistro with lots of new ideas on offer. Specialities include fine country dishes from Burgundy, game in season and seafood including bouillabaisse with langoustines. Closed Saturday lunch and Sunday.

Chez la Vieille

37 Rue de l'Arbre Sec, 75001
Tel. 42 60 15 78

The 'old woman' in the name of this establishment is Adrienne Biasin who presided over the kitchen for several decades. Young successors continue to produce her style of French home cooking at its best: terrines, savoury tarts, calf's liver and beef with carrots. Open at lunch-time only. Closed Saturday, Sunday and August.

Chiberta

3 Rue Arsène-Houssaye, 75008
Tel. 45 63 77 90

This elegant restaurant just beside l'Etoile has a very faithful local clientele. Closed Saturday, Sunday, all August and holidays. Chef Philippe da Silva's style is classical haute cuisine.

Conti

72 Rue Lauriston, 75116
Tel. 47 27 74 67

The chef here, formerly with the celebrated Troisgros brothers in Roanne, is noted for his interpretations of Italian dishes – working wonders with pasta. Closed Saturday, Sunday and public holidays.

Copenhague ▌▌

142 Avenue des Champs-Elysées, 75008
Tel. 44 13 86 26
Close to l'Etoile, this restaurant serves Danish and other Scandinavian specialities, including game and reindeer. Closed Sunday and August. The Flora Danica delicatessen and snack bar downstairs is less formal and open daily.

La Brasserie Fauchon ▌▌

26-30 Place de la Madeleine, 75008
Tel. 47 42 60 11
The best known quality food shop in Paris offers a choice of restaurants on its premises. Look round the store to sharpen your appetite beforehand. Closed Sunday.

La Fermette Marbeuf ▌▌

5 Rue Marbeuf, 75008
Tel. 47 20 63 53
Worth a visit for the art nouveau setting in the back room, with ceramics and cast-iron columns, as well as for the food, emphasizing the finest fresh farm produce. Open daily.

Flo ▌

7 Cour des Petites Ecuries, 75010
Tel. 47 70 13 59
The fame of this traditional brasserie in a little back street has spread: now it runs branches in various parts of Paris. The original serves good seafood, Alsace specialities and brasserie standards. Budget menu after 10 30pm. Open every day until 1.30am.

Le Grand Véfour ▌▌▌▌

17 Rue de Beaujolais, 75001
Tel. 42 96 56 27
Set in a gorgeously ornate late 18th-century salon in the Palais-Royal, where Napoleon once took dinner with Josephine. In contrast Guy Martin's cuisine is modern, light and imaginative. Closed Saturday, Sunday and August.

Guyvonne ▌▌▌

14 Rue de Thann, 75017
Tel. 42 27 25 43
Guy Cros likes to cook fish, and you can choose from six or seven kinds on the menu, depending on arrivals. Offal and country fare are also worth noting. Closed Saturday and Sunday.

Le Manoir de Paris ▌▌▌

6 Rue Pierre-Demours, 75017
Tel. 45 72 25 25
A delightful Belle Epoque setting for contemporary cuisine. Upstairs La Niçoise serves delicious Provençal dishes in a substantially lower price range. Closed Saturday lunch-time and Sunday.

Café Marly

Palais du Louvre,
93 Rue de Rivoli, 75001
Tel. 49 26 06 60
You can rest from your labours in the Louvre in these Second Empire style rooms, facing the pyramid or the skylit Cour Louvre. Snacks, lunch and dinner served. Open daily from 8am to 2am.

Brasserie du Café de la Paix

12 Blvd des Capucins, 75009
Tel. 40 07 30 20
Traditional brasserie food, cheerfully served in the remarkable and historic setting of this 1862 café; vast, gilded and mirrored, adjoining a covered terrace opposite the Opéra-Garnier. Open daily.

Le Perroquet Vert

7 Rue Cavalotti, 75018
Tel. 45 22 49 16
A casual bistro which has been a Montmartre institution for over a century, serving simple country food at an economy price. Closed Saturday lunch-time and Sunday.

Pharamond

24 Rue Grande-Truanderie,
75001
Tel. 42 33 06 72
In an authentic Belle Epoque setting, this restaurant serves a range

of fine Normandy cuisine, turning the lowliest offal and giblets as well as great seafood into divine dishes. Closed Sunday, and Monday lunch-time.

Au Pied de Cochon

6 Rue Coquillière, 75001
Tel. 42 36 11 75
Bright and cheerful restaurant and terrace, in the Les Halles quarter, open 24 hours every day. Specialities are fish, big seafood platters and pigs' trotters stuffed with truffle pâté as well as budget priced set menus.

RIGHT BANK – EAST (3-4, 10-12)

Benoît

20 Rue St.-Martin, 75004
Tel. 42 72 25 76
Traditional cuisine *bourgeoise* in a real bistro that has barely changed since its foundation in 1912. This is a popular place and you need to book days in advance. Closed Saturday, Sunday and August.

Au Châteaubriant

23 Rue de Chabrol, 75010
Tel. 48 24 58 94
The French poet Jacques Prévert was a regular here, and the décor is enhanced by fine paintings. The cooking is Italian-influenced with

77

seafood pastas a speciality. Closed Sunday, Monday and August.

Chez Julien

1 Rue Pont Louis-Philippe, 75004
Tel. 42 78 31 64
A friendly family-run bistro in a 19th-century bakery, with home-style food. Closed Saturday lunch, Sunday and Monday lunch.

Dos de la Baleine

40 Rue des Blancs Manteaux, 75004
Tel. 42 73 38 98
A little restaurant in the Marais run by two cheerful chefs offering interpretations of country cooking at very reasonable prices. Closed Saturday lunch and Sunday.

Brasserie l'Européen

21bis Blvd Diderot, 75012
Tel. 43 43 99 70
Specializes in shellfish, especially oysters in season, but also snacks and bistro standards in the Bastille area. Open daily 11am to 1am.

Le Café Moderne

19 Rue Keller, 75011
Tel. 47 00 53 62
A young team in an old bistro offers heart-warming cuisine, such as black pudding and Morteau sausage, as well as lighter fare like salmon tartare. Closed Sunday.

Terminus Nord–Brasserie 1925

23 Rue de Dunkerque, 75010
Tel. 42 85 05 15
In the fine 19th-century building facing the Gare du Nord, a classic brasserie, noted for its seafood and Alsace country cooking. Open daily from 11am until 12 30am.

Les Voyageurs

1 Rue Keller, 75011
Tel. 48 05 86 14
Grilled fish and shellfish at reasonable prices are the specialities of this friendly restaurant near Place de la Bastille. Closed Saturday lunch-time and Sunday evening.

LEFT BANK (5-7, 14-15)

Le Bistrot de Paris

33 Rue de Lille, 75007
Tel. 42 61 16 83
1900-style bistro, with a lovely billiard room on the first floor. Owner Michel Olivier (a TV chef) lives up to his excellent reputation. Closed Saturday lunch-time and Sunday. Book well ahead.

Le Bistrot d'André

232 Rue Saint-Charles, 75015
Tel. 45 57 89 14
This used to be the local bistro for the workers of André Citroën's car factory; it belonged to the great

Major Museums

The Louvre

Far less daunting and stuffy since its facelift, the Musée du Louvre is still formidable for its sheer size. In 1793 when the leaders of the Revolution declared the palace a national museum, it held 630 works of art; a recent inventory listed 250,000. Don't be put off – it's an exhilarating experience just attempting to come to grips with such vast collections of painting and sculpture – with artefacts from 5000BC to 1848 (the date at which the Musée d'Orsay takes over).

Whatever you might think of it, the glass **pyramid** designed by Chinese-American architect I.M. Pei provides a striking modern entrance. You descend by escalator to the reception area, which comprises

The glass pyramid makes a focus for the Louvre and lights its underground reception area.

shops, cafés and the ticket office. At the information counter, collect a copy of the free **handbook** with colour-coded floor plans.

Broad corridors lead to the various parts of the museum. The museum authorities have made heroic efforts to help you find your way through the labyrinth. Each of the three main wings is named after one of France's great figures: the Richelieu wing, the Sully wing in the east and the Denon wing beside the Seine. Each wing is then divided into numbered areas, which are shown on the colour floor plans. The locations of some of the most famous exhibits are pin-pointed. You *will* get lost at times, but in doing so you may discover unlooked-for marvels.

A good way to tackle the museum is to spend an initial half-day seeing the highlights. For this, you may find an 'acoustiguide' (recorded tour) helpful. Look out for some of the following highlights.

Medieval moat: the 12th-century fortress' foundations and drawbridge support.

Egyptian: the lion-headed *Sekhmet* (1400 BC) and the huge *Amenophis IV* (1370 BC).

Greek: the winged *Victory of Samothrace* and beautifully proportioned *Vénus de Milo*.

Italian: the splendid sculpture of the *Two Slaves* by Michelangelo; Leonardo da Vinci's fabled *Mona Lisa* (*La Joconde*), and also his sublime *Virgin of the Rocks*; Titian's voluptuous *Woman at her Toilet*; the poignant *Old Man and His Grandson* by Ghirlandaio.

French: Poussin's *Arcadian Shepherds*; Watteau's hypnotically melancholy *Gilles* and graceful *Embarkation for Cythera*; Fragonard's erotic *Le Verrou* (*The Bolt*), Delacroix's *Liberty Guiding the People* and Courbet's piercing study of provincial bourgeoisie, *Funeral at Ornans*.

Dutch and Flemish: Rembrandt's cheerful *Self-Portrait with a Toque*, his beloved *Hendrickje Stoffels*, also portrayed nude in *Bathesheba Bathing*; Van Dyke's gracious, dignified *Charles I of England*; among scores of 'official' Rubens, his tender *Helena Fourment*.

*T*he Musée d'Orsay is a fitting exhibition space for some of the world's best known works of art.

Spanish: the uncompromising Velázquez portrait of *Queen Marianna of Austria*; El Greco's mystic *Christ on the Cross*; Ribera's gruesomely good-humoured *The Club Foot* (*Le Pied-Bot*).

German: a gripping *Self-Portrait* by Dürer; Holbein's *Erasmus*.

English: *Conversation in a Park* by Gainsborough.

Musée d'Orsay

'The station is superb and truly looks like a Fine Arts Museum, and since the Fine Arts Museum resembles a station, I suggest ... we make the change while we still can,' joked the painter Edouard Detaille in 1900. In 1986 that was more or less what happened. Facing the Tuileries gardens across the river, the converted 19th-century hotel-cum-railway station was transformed into the impressive Musée d'Orsay, devoted to French art from 1848 to 1914. In effect, it carries on where the Louvre leaves off. Keeping the exterior much as it was, Italian architect Gae Aulenti adapted the interior to house many of the previously scattered works of that period, including the magnificent Impressionist collections formerly held in the Jeu de Paume. Sculpture is well represented, and photography is present from its inception (1839). **83**

It is one of the easiest of great museums to navigate: the free floor plan is crystal clear, and so are the signs. There are mesmerizing arrays of work by Renoir, Cézanne, Manet, Monet (including five of his studies of Rouen Cathedral in various lights) and van Gogh, (the best collection outside the van Gogh Museum in Amsterdam, with several of the pictures from his frenzied period of activity in the months before his death in 1890).

Both layout and lighting are astonishing; every part of the old terminus has been used in a highly imaginative way and frequent lectures, guided tours and concerts are scheduled. When you need a break, there is a café high up behind a huge clock, and on the middle level the former station hotel's restaurant, beautifully restored, is a restaurant again.

The inside-out design of the Pompidou Centre creates a fine backdrop for street performers.

Centre Georges Pompidou (Beaubourg)

'That'll get them screaming,' said the President of the time, Georges Pompidou, as he approved the plans (chosen from 681 competing designs) for the Centre National de l'Art Contemporain, later named Centre Georges Pompidou and occasionally known as Beaubourg after the 13th-century neighbourhood surrounding it.

Its combination of public library, children's workshop and special library, *cinémathèque*, industrial design centre and a music laboratory makes the complex a constant hive of activity, with free shows and a rendezvous point outside. The excellent **National Museum of Modern Art** on the 4th and then 3rd floors (in that order, and simple to follow with the free map) provides a rewarding education in all the disparate art movements of the 20th century, from the Fauve to Cubism to Abstract Expressionism, Dadaism, Surrealism and all the breakaway factions and reactions which followed them. The great innovators are all lined up for your perusal here: Matisse, Picasso, Kandinsky, Léger, Dubuffet, Pollock and sculptors Brancusi, Arp and Giacommetti.

The 3rd floor takes up the story of ever-increasing fragmentation and experiment, and continues it almost to the present day. The 5th floor stages temporary exhibitions: there's also a restaurant with a wonderful view.

Musée de l'Orangerie

A pavilion in the corner of the Tuileries gardens is home to the outstanding Jean Walther-Paul Guillaume Collection. By the terms of their wills, the legacy had to stay here, otherwise it might have been moved to the Musée d'Orsay. Masterpieces by Cézanne, Renoir, Utrillo, Rousseau, Modigliani, Picasso, Derain and Soutine hang in the upstairs rooms. Guillaume himself knew most of the artists and several of them did portraits of him. The walls of the two oval rooms downstairs are almost completely covered by huge murals of waterlilies (*Nymphéas*) which Monet painted as a gift to the nation.

Musée Picasso

Over 200 paintings, 158 sculptures and hundreds of drawings, engravings, ceramics and models for stage sets and costumes from Picasso's private collections were given to the nation by his heirs, in lieu of taxes owed on his death. The **85** museum includes the artist's own collection of works by fellow painters Braque, Matisse, Miró, Degas, Renoir and Rousseau. In addition, a number of intriguing private relics are displayed: letters, photo albums, bullfight tickets and holiday postcards.

The finely detailed Lady with the Unicorn *tapestries are works of intriguing symbolism.*

Musée National du Moyen Age (Musée de Cluny)

The setting is amazing, an old abbey which incorporated the massive remains of the city's 3rd-century Roman baths, the Thermes de Cluny. One of the exhibits is older still: the fragments of a monument to Jupiter (probably 1st century AD) discovered near Notre-Dame. Twenty-one of the 28 heads of the kings of Judah from Notre-

Dame (see p.28) were found in a bank vault and are now here – notice that some retain traces of colouring. But the most celebrated treasures of all at this museum are the late 15th-century **tapestries**, especially the set known as the *Lady with the Unicorn*, depicting the five senses. Even if you think you have no interest in tapestries, these very delicate, intricate and mysterious scenes will impress you.

Parc de la Villette: Cité des Sciences

If there's one thing this institution dislikes, it's being called a museum. First, the Parc de la Villette offers a whole range of activities, and second, it puts the accent firmly on participation. But as with any good museum, you can learn a lot and enjoy yourself too. There's something for all ages, and for anyone ready to be excited by the world of science.

The main building has a lot in common with Beaubourg – although this one is four times bigger. A variety of themes are explored: space, health, communications, agriculture, etc. Some of the hands-on displays are fun, but you need to understand French to follow all the information presented.

The sizeable stainless-steel Géode sphere, made of 6,433 reflecting triangles, houses a cinema with a 360° movie screen 36m (118ft) in diameter. As you watch the film, you feel as if you're part of it. There's also a 60-seat space-flight simulator. The principal exhibition area, the planetarium, aquarium and submarine *Argonaute* are covered by the entry fee (or Museum Pass), but all other activities are extra – even the creative play areas for young children – and fairly expensive. (See also p.89.)

A canal passes right through the park, so you can reach it by boat from central Paris (a three-hour trip, see p.22). The nearby **Cité de la Musique**, on the other side of the canal, has a new concert hall, the ultra modern buildings of the Conservatoire National (music academy) and an impressively large rock venue, the Zénith. **87**

Museums

Entry charges range from 25 to 50F. In some museums, under-18s enter free, with 18-25s and over-60s paying half price. In others, under-7s are free, 7-17s pay a reduced rate. Some museums charge less on Sundays.

The **Museum Pass** (*Carte Musées et Monuments*) gives entry to 65 museums and monuments in Paris and its region, including the Louvre and Versailles. Passes are valid for one, three or five consecutive days and can be bought at museum ticket offices, tourist offices and main métro stations. You'll make a saving if you visit just two museums per day (even fewer for the 5-day pass). When buying your ticket make sure you get the free booklet detailing all the museums you can visit with your pass.

Paris is home to countless museums and you'll be faced with difficult choices. These are some of the most important:

Musée du Louvre (The Louvre), the vast palace with huge collections, especially ancient Egyptian, Greek and Roman art, and European painting up to 1848. Open 9am-6pm (Napoleon Hall 10pm); closed Tuesday. Métro: Palais-Royal-Musée du Louvre. (See p.81)

Musée d'Orsay, the brilliantly converted former railway station is the home of a breathtaking collection of European art, especially French, from 1848 to 1914. Open 9am-6pm (summer and Sunday in winter); 10am-6pm (winter); Thursdays to 9.45pm; closed Monday. Métro: Solférino, (RER Musée d'Orsay). (See p.83)

Centre Georges Pompidou (Musée National d'Art Moderne), this extraordinary building befits a collection featuring 20th-century art in all its eccentric variety. Open noon-10pm; weekends and public holidays 10am-10pm; closed Tuesday and 1 May. Métro: Rambuteau, Hôtel-de-Ville, Châtelet. (See p.84)

Musée d'Art Moderne de la Ville de Paris, a 20th-century collection to rival the Pompidou Centre's, and fewer crowds. It is especially strong on Braque, Matisse, Utrillo, Dufy, Delauney and Chagall. The monumental 1937 Palais de Tokio is an exhibit in its own right. Open 10am-5.45pm; closed Monday. Métro: Iéna, Alma-Marceau.

Musée de l'Homme, in the 1937 Palais de Chaillot, huge collections of fossils, prehistoric artefacts, world-wide ethnology. Open 9.45am-5.15pm; closed Tuesday. Métro: Trocadéro.

Musée National du Moyen Age (Musée de Cluny), art of the Middle Ages, in the broadest sense, from 1st-century Roman to around 1500, housed in an old abbey, and the massive remains of the Roman baths. Open 9.15am-5.45pm; closed Tuesday. Métro: Saint-Michel, Cluny, Maubert-Mutualité. (See p.86)

Musée de l'Orangerie, a pavilion in the corner of the Tuileries gardens, with Monet murals and the superb Walther-Guillaume Collection of Impressionist and post-Impressionist art. Open 9.45am-5.15pm; closed Tuesday. Métro: Concorde. (See p.85)

Musée Rodin, a fine 18th-century mansion and its garden, with the definitive collection of works by the great sculptor. Open 10am-5.45pm (5pm, October-March); closed Monday. Métro: Varenne.

Musée Picasso, the artist's collection of his own work, as well as many pictures by his friends and contemporaries, in a fine old house and garden in the Marais. Open 9.30am-6pm (5.30pm, winter); closed Tuesday. Métro: Chemin Vert, Saint-Paul. (See p.85)

Palais de la Découverte, mainly intended for a young audience, with plenty of hands-on exhibits about science and exploration, as well as a planetarium. Open 9.30am-6pm; Sunday 10am-7pm; closed Monday. Métro: Champs-Elysées-Clémenceau, Franklin-Roosevelt.

Musée Carnavalet (Musée de l'Histoire de Paris), documents, engravings and paintings bring Paris' history to life. In an outstanding exhibit devoted to the Revolution, a letter from Robespierre is dramatically stained with the author's blood: he was arrested and wounded while signing it. Open 10am-5.40pm; closed Monday. Métro: Saint-Paul, Chemin Vert, Bastille.

Cité des Sciences et de l'Industrie (La Villette), in a vast park on the north-eastern outskirts, exhibitions with plenty of audio-visual and interactive displays, 3D and 360° films and much more, designed to educate and entertain. Open 10am-6pm; Sunday 7pm; closed Monday. Métro: Porte de la Villette. (See p.87)

Excursions

Chartres

Built around the year 1200, Chartres Cathedral is visible from far away, towering above the old town and the surrounding plain. Its medieval stained glass, including three fine rose windows, is of unrivalled complexity and stunning beauty. Climb to the roof for the extraordinary view of the stonework and flying buttresses.

Situated 88km (55 miles) southwest of Paris by the A11 or N10, or by train from Gare Montparnasse. A large number of companies run bus tours from Paris. Open 7am-7.30pm daily (7.30am-7pm October-March). The crypt and tower, and sometimes the cathedral itself, may be closed 1-2pm.

Fontainebleau

Many visitors find the château more appealing and certainly less daunting than Versailles. It was a royal palace for much longer, with certain additions made over seven centuries, notably by François I in the 16th century. The adjoining town is charming and the surrounding forest, cool and shaded even in the hottest summer, is perfect for gentle walks, cycle rides and picnics.

Situated 64km (40 miles) southeast of Paris by the A6 or

Fontainebleau was a favourite residence for many French rulers, from François I to Napoleon.

by train from Gare de Lyon and then bus to the château. Bus tours from Paris are available. Open 9.30am-12.30pm, 2-5pm. Closed Tuesday.

Giverny

These magnificent floral and water gardens were laid out by Claude Monet who lived in Giverny from 1883 to 1926. He painted them many times, especially the waterlilies.

Situated 85km (53 miles) northwest of Paris by the A13, D181 and D5, or by train from Gare St-Lazare to Vernon. The house is open April-October, 10am-noon, 2-6pm. The gardens are open all year, 10am-6pm. Closed Monday.

Malmaison

Set in lovely grounds, the château used to be the home of Napoleon's wife, the Empress Josephine, who continued to live here after their divorce. Many of her possessions are on display in the various private and state apartments open to visitors.

Located 6km (4 miles) west of Paris. Métro: Grande Arche de La Défense, then bus 258, or RER to Rueil-Malmaison, and then walk. Open 10.30am-noon, 1.30-5.30pm (4.30pm in winter). Closed Tuesday.

Vaux-le-Vicomte

A splendid 17th-century château and gardens designed by Le Vau, Le Nôtre and Le Brun for Louis XIV's finance minister, Fouquet. No sooner was the magnificent project completed than the king had its owner arrested for embezzlement and jailed for life.

Situated 56km (35 miles) southeast of Paris on the N5, or by train from Gare de Lyon to Melun, and then taxi. Open daily 10am-6pm (11am-5pm November-March). Closed in January.

Versailles

Louis XIV, 'the Sun King', was quite simply a megalomaniac, but he also had extraordinary vision. He was wary of Paris and its rabble (all too **91** easily roused) and rising aristocracy (ever-demanding and arrogant). What better way to keep potential trouble-makers under his thumb than to coop them up at Versailles, and let them squabble for rights and privileges as futile as attending His Majesty's awakening?

Versailles is as extravagant, formidable and vainglorious as the man himself. Louis XIII had hoped to turn his favourite hunting ground into a modest retirement home, but his son and heir made it the centre of a universe, proclaiming his own grandeur in an edifice of brick, marble, gilt and crystal.

A visit to the château takes most or all of a day, entails a lot of walking and shouldn't be inflicted on young children. Bus tours leave from the Tuileries gardens on the Rue de Rivoli side but you may prefer to do things in your own time. Make an early start, travel by RER (see p.24) and you can fit in a morning tour of part of the palace; stroll through the gardens; have lunch beside the Grand Canal (a packed lunch allows you to avoid Versailles'

tourist traps); take tea in the grounds of the Petit Trianon; and finally wander back across the palace gardens for a last view of the château at sunset.

The central section of the building (where the royal family lived) was conceived by Louis Le Vau, Jules Hardouin-Mansart and landscape designer André Le Nôtre in 1661. It was completed 21 years later. Le Vau also designed the marble courtyard, decorated with 84 marble busts.

Highlights of the vast interior include the **Royal Chapel**, a gem of high Baroque; the **State Apartments** in which Louis XIV used to entertain; the Salon de Diane, where he would try his hand at billiards – since it didn't go down well to beat a Sun King, he generally won; the glittering **Hall of Mirrors** (*Galerie des Glaces*), 73m (240ft) long and built to catch the setting sun in 17 tall, arched panels of mirrors. Adjoining it is the King's bedroom, where Louis died of gangrene of the leg in 1715. In the Queen's bedroom, 19 royal children were born, the births often attended by members of the public, as was the custom. Several parts of the château, including Louis XV's superb **Royal Opera**, have to be visited on separate guided tours.

The most impressive façade faces west, to the gardens; the pretty fountains begin to play at 3.30pm on three Sundays a month, from May to September. You should also look at the **Grand Trianon**, the small palace that Louis XIV used on occasions when he wanted to get away from the château,

the **Petit Trianon** favoured by Louis XV, and the marvellous **Hameau** (little village) and miniature farm where Marie-Antoinette, queen of Louis XVI, famously played at the simple life. They're some way from the château and each other: a little train runs a shuttle service, at a price.

The enormous courtyard of Versailles contains a statue of its creator, Louis XIV, the 'Sun King'.

Versailles is situated 24km (15 miles) southwest of Paris, by road (N10); or by train from Gare St-Lazare to Versailles; or by RER (line C5) to Versailles-Rive Gauche; or by métro to Pont de Sèvres, then bus 171. The château is open 9am-6.30pm (winter 5.30pm); the Grand and Petit Trianon 10am-6.30pm (10am-12.30pm and 2-5.30pm Tuesday-Friday, 10am-5.30pm Saturday and Sunday in winter); the gardens 7am-sunset. Closed Monday.

Disneyland Paris

Much more then a theme park, Disney's ambitious recreation complex also encompasses hotels, camping facilities, restaurants, a convention centre, a championship golf course, tennis courts and several swimming pools.

In the theme park itself, Main Street USA, recapturing the traditions of small-town America at the turn of the century, leads to four other 'lands' – Frontierland, Adventureland, Fantasyland and Discoveryland. Each themed section has a variety of fun experiences on offer, from old-fashioned fairground rides to roller coasters, a water-splash, shows and souvenir shops. Hosts Mickey and Minnie Mouse, Goofy, Donald Duck and Pluto wander around in their familiar costumes, posing with visitors but never speaking – which avoids language problems. Every day at 3pm there's a spectacular all-singing, all-dancing parade including floats inspired by the famous Disney movies.

The Berlitz POCKET GUIDE TO DISNEYLAND PARIS (still frequently called by its earlier name of Euro-Disney) gives full details of the resort. For further information about day-to-day happenings there, telephone (1) 64 74 30 00.

Situated 32km (20 miles) east of Paris, close by Marne-la-Vallée. A motorway (*autoroute*) gives access from the city and the airports, Charles-de-Gaulle and Orly. Speedy commuter trains (RER line A) from the capital and even faster long-distance trains (TGV) serve Marne-la-Vallée/Chessy station near the entrance.

What to Do

If you can take the time off from sightseeing, the shopping mix is unique, ranging from high fashion and small specialist shops to flea markets. You'll probably get enough exercise from all the walking you'll be doing, but plenty of facilities exist for both fitness fanatics and sports spectating. Eating out (see p.106) is perhaps the number one evening diversion, and street life the best free show. In terms of organized entertainment, Paris is still in love with the movies, and the music scene is especially diverse.

Shopping

The majority of shops and department stores are open from 9am to 7pm, Tuesday to Saturday. Some shops close at lunch-time from noon till 2pm and many are closed on Monday mornings, if not all day Monday. The first to open their doors are usually the bakeries (*boulangerie*), and there's always a small grocer (*épicerie*) or mini-supermarket in which you can shop till 9 or 10pm, or even midnight. On Sundays, too, you are never stuck, even if food shops tend to close at midday. The Drugstore at the top of the Champs-Elysées is open until 2am every night for

The streets and lanes of Paris are a paradise for anyone who enjoys shopping.

In Galeries Lafayette, don't miss the gorgeous art nouveau glass dome, dating from 1900.

snacks, takeaways, books, assorted gifts and essentials.

Department Stores. The old Galeries Lafayette on Boulevard Haussmann stocks a wide range of clothes at all price levels. Fashion shows are held at 11am on Wednesdays and also Fridays in summer. The china department is huge, and the cosmetics, sportswear and luggage sections excellent. **Au Printemps**, just next door, has the biggest selection of shoes and is famous for its lingerie, toys and innovative household goods. Fashion shows are at 10am on Tuesdays as well as Fridays in summer.

FNAC belongs to the newer, younger generation of department stores. Branches at l'Etoile, Montparnasse and the Forum des Halles, as well as La Défense, have selections of books, discount CDs and cassettes, electronics and sports goods. **Virgin Megastore**, on the Champs-Elysées, has an even bigger stock of CDs.

Marks & Spencers and **C&A** have Paris branches, but more typically French are the established **Au Bon Marché** at Sèvres-Babylone and **La Samaritaine** opposite Pont-Neuf (at 75 Rue de Rivoli), where you'll find everything from home furnishings to pets, and a splendid view of the city from its 10th-floor terrace.

The large modern **shopping malls** include the Forum des Halles, Centre Maine-Montparnasse and the Palais des Congrès at Porte Maillot.

Fashion and Accessories. Almost synonymous with chic style, Paris remains paramount in the fashion stakes, despite hot competition. Most of the *couture* houses are concentrated on the Right Bank close by the Rue du Faubourg-Saint-Honoré (just 'Le Faubourg' to regular shoppers) and classier Avenue Montaigne where designers Christian Lacroix, Karl Lagerfeld, Hermès, Christian Dior, Yves Saint Laurent and Gianni Versace, to name a few, have shops. From here and over to Les Halles and Place des Victoires, the *haute couture* houses and ready-to-wear (*prêt-à-porter*) boutiques have spread to the Left Bank around Saint-Germain-des-Prés.

Stores such as Dorothée-Bis, Benetton and the less expensive, but lower quality Tati

---

VAT Exemption

Visitors from outside the European Union can claim exemption from sales taxes (*TVA*) if they spend more than 2,000F on purchases from a single shop: the sum can be made up of various items. EU residents do not qualify. Department stores and luxury goods shops are used to dealing with foreign visitors. Staff will provide a form, *bordereau de vente* (export sales invoice): you then have it stamped by customs as you leave France or the EU and mail it back to the store to reclaim the tax. The shop eventually sends you a refund in French francs.

Nostalgia is the keynote in stalls by the Seine, selling prints, old magazines and postcards.

African and Polynesian art, as well as Louis XV, Second Empire, art nouveau and art deco. Across the river, 250 dealers are concentrated in the Louvre des Antiquaires, by the Place du Palais-Royal, closed Monday (and Sunday in July and August), and others are scattered around Les Halles.

Flea Markets (*Marchés aux Puces*). There's virtually no chance of picking up a treasure that has slipped through the hands of the experts, but it's fun to try. Many of the stands are run by professional dealers. The giant of the flea markets is Saint-Ouen at the Porte de Clignancourt, 75018, open from about 6am to 7pm, Saturday, Sunday and Monday. The market at Porte de Vanves, 75014, has a high proportion of junk and sees fewer tourists (open Saturday and Sunday

are found throughout the capital; there's a branch at Barbès-Rochechouart but be prepared to jostle. Children's clothes are fun and stylish too, though you may balk at the prices. Try chains such as Jacadi or Tartine et Chocolat.

Antiques. Antique shops cluster around the Left Bank's 6th and 7th *arrondissements*. The Carré des Antiquaires, a little rectangle bounded by the Quai Voltaire, the Boulevard Saint-Germain, the Rues du Bac and des Saints-Pères, is something of a museum of ancient Egyptian, Chinese, pre-Columbian,

6am-6pm). You'll find bric-a-brac and old or second-hand clothes at Porte de Montreuil, 75020, open Saturday, Sunday and Monday mornings. For inexpensive new clothes, pay a visit to the Carreau du Temple, 75003, open every morning except Monday.

Books. Trade in old and new books flourishes on the Left Bank in or around the Latin Quarter, notably at the Odéon. Second-hand bookshops, commonly known as *bouquinistes*, line the quays of the Seine, especially between Pont Saint-Michel and Pont des Arts. It's worth rummaging through the mass of books, prints, postcards and periodicals for occasional finds, though the asking prices may seem high.

An extraordinary collection of new art books is available at the bookshop below the Pyramide du Louvre. The Pompidou Centre's bookshop isn't bad either.

If you're pining for English-language books try Brentano's at 37 Avenue de l'Opéra, W.H. Smith at 248 Rue de Rivoli, or the NQL (Nouveau Quartier Latin) at the top of Boulevard Saint-Michel.

Food and Drink. Fine foods can make wonderful presents. Thanks to today's packaging methods, it's possible to transport goods that previously spoiled en route (but remember the bans on most food imports imposed by the US and Australia, among others). Two famous luxury grocery shops, **Fauchon** and **Hédiard**, glare at each other across the Place de la Madeleine. For **wines**, the Nicolas chain has a wide range at its 150 Paris branches. A bigger selection is at Legrand, on Rue de la Banque. Spirits (liquor) and liqueurs may be less expensive at the duty-free shops as you leave France, though note that the choice will be more limited.

Food Markets. Covered markets or street markets in the old style operate all over Paris, but especially the Left Bank. Try the photogenic Rue de Buci in St-Germain-des-Prés, open every morning except **99**

In spite of inroads made by the supermarkets, many Parisians still shop for food at market stalls.

Monday, or Rue de la Convention in Montparnasse, near the Convention métro station, on Tuesday, Thursday and Sunday mornings.

If you want to visit only one, try **Rue Mouffetard**, behind the Panthéon, especially on Tuesday, Thursday or Saturday morning. You could be in a country village: stalls and shops are piled with mouth-watering displays of food. Explore the side streets at the lower end where the African market stalls are stocked with dried fish and baskets, spices, dried fruit and nuts, and hawkers sell out of crates and sacks.

The **flower** market in Place Lepine, near Notre-Dame on Ile de la Cité, opens from 8am to 7.30pm daily. On Sundays, it switches to small pets, especially cage birds. The flower stalls in Place de la Madeleine open daily except Monday.

Sports

Check the fashion images: fitness is sexy, so many Parisians are prepared to work at it. You can join them in *le jogging* or *le footing* (both mean jogging) in the big parks of the Bois de Boulogne and Bois de Vincennes, along the quays beside the Seine, in the Tuileries gardens and even by the Champs-Elysées. More of a challenge are the hilly Parc Montsouris (on the Left Bank) or Buttes-Chaumont (on the Right). An alternative is to hire a **bicycle** (see p.117). Ask at tourist offices for information on bike tours of the city and outlying areas such as Fontainebleau.

There are a number of public **tennis** courts in Paris, but it's first-come-first-serve, as at the Jardin du Luxembourg courts. Big hotels may arrange for their guests to play at one of the many tennis clubs.

Municipal pools are available for **swimming**. The most serious action takes place at the Olympic-size indoor pool of the Centre de Natation, at 34 Boulevard Carnot.

Among **spectator sports**, pride of place goes to **horse-racing**. The summer meetings at Longchamp (venue of the 'Prix de l'Arc de Triomphe') Auteuil and Chantilly are as elegant as Britain's Ascot. The serious punter who wants to avoid the frills and champagne can have a very good time at Vincennes and Enghien, at the trotting races.

Rugby and **football** (soccer) can be seen at the modern stadium of Parc-des-Princes.

Trotting races are a favourite Parisian spectator sport – and an excuse for a bet. **101**

Tennis tournaments usually take place at Roland-Garros. (Both of these venues are at the southern end of the Bois de Boulogne.) The Palais Omnisports de Paris-Bercy, just beside the Gare de Lyon, was designed for a variety of sports and stages everything from rock concerts to tango competitions, as well as cycle races and indoor windsurfing.

Entertainment

To see what's on in Paris while you are there, buy one of the weekly guides, *Pariscope* or *L'Officiel des Spectacles*, with comprehensive listings of all kinds of entertainment.

The cinema is a great national passion, with 300 different **films** showing every week in the capital. For undubbed versions with French subtitles, look out for the letters VO (*version originale*) in the listings or posters.

Keeping up with the latest in **discos** and **clubs** can be a full-time job for professional night-owls: there's no point in turning up before midnight. Many are nominally private, which means you only get in if the doormen like the way you look and think you're going to spend. Some expensive, exclusive examples hide out around the Champs-Elysées, such as Régine's in the Rue de Ponthieu. Louder, less expensive, younger and weirder places come and go around Bastille and Les Halles. There's still some life in Saint-Germain-des-Prés and the Latin Quarter, especially in university term time – making local friends is the best way to find it.

Pop and rock concerts are held at the spectacular Zénith in the Cité de la Musique (La Villette, métro Porte de Pantin) and also sometimes at Parc-des-Princes (métro: Porte de St-Cloud).

The French take their **jazz** seriously, and Paris has many jazz clubs. The New Morning (Rue des Petites-Ecuries) attracts the big American and European musicians, while Le Dunois (Rue Dunois) is an intimate place, cultivating more avant-garde music. The Lionel

Hampton club at the Méridien Etoile (Porte Maillot) has a full programme of guest performers. The old-established Caveau de la Huchette (Rue de la Huchette in St-Germain-des-Prés) opens every night at 9.30pm for listening and dancing to a small combo or big band swing or bebop. Entrance prices of around 60-120F may include your first drink; extra drinks cost 30-60F.

In the realm of **classical music**, Paris has come back into its own, with many fine concerts, the National Opera at the modern Opéra-Bastille, and the National Ballet at the restored Opéra-Garnier. In all cases, some seats are reasonably priced though they tend to go quickly. Look out for free concerts in churches.

Modern **dance** is enjoying a revival, with a new wave of

*T*wo great, ornate institutions face Place de l'Opéra, the Café de la Paix and Opéra-Garnier.

small, imaginative companies beginning modestly enough at the Café de la Danse (Passage Louis-Philippe), Théâtre Garnier and Centre Pompidou, before reaching the heights of the Théâtre de la Bastille.

With some command of the French language, **theatre** lovers can enjoy the classics by Molière, Racine or Corneille at the Comédie Française (Rue de Richelieu) and contemporary plays at other theatres.

The naughty image of Paris has a long history and isn't dead yet. The Folies Bergères (Rue Richer), which launched the careers of Josephine Baker, Mistinguett and Maurice Chevalier, and the Lido on the Champs-Elysées are both classic survivors. The most famous modern-day floor show, chic as well as erotic and brilliantly choreographed, is at the Crazy Horse Saloon (Avenue George V). Toulouse-Lautrec painted the showgirls of the Moulin Rouge (Place Blanche) a century ago, and it still puts on a boisterous floor show in the old tradition, though mainly for the busloads of tourists nowadays. The rest of Pigalle plumbs the lower depths with a certain glee that continues to fascinate visitors.

Finally, the least expensive evening entertainment is people-watching: a coffee or beer at a café terrace can go a surprisingly long way. The streets stay busy into the small hours but take a bit of care; drugs have given a grimmer edge to the late night scene.

Paris for Children

From dawn to dusk, a lot of the activities that interest adults are fortunately likely to appeal to children as well. Boat trips (see p.22) especially are good fun for everyone. The **Jardin d'Acclimatation** in the Bois de Boulogne (see p.63) is a special children's park, complete with a small zoo, pony rides, puppet shows and other attractions (open daily, 10am-6pm). The capital's main zoo, open daily, 9am-5.30pm (6pm during summer), is located in the Bois de Vincennes (Porte Dorée métro station).

Small children are bound to enjoy the merry-go-round and pony rides in the **Jardin du Luxembourg**, where they can also watch the toy boats capsize in the fountain. A broad range of activities goes on at the **Centre Pompidou**, including art workshops for children (*Atelier des Enfants*) on Wednesday and Saturday afternoons; tel. (1) 44 78 40 36. For the scientifically minded, there's a great deal to learn painlessly at the Cité des Sciences et de l'Industrie at **La Villette** (see p.87). The **Palais de la Découverte** (see p.89) makes use of a similar hands-on approach.

Some 30km (20 miles) outside Paris at Marne-la-Vallée, the **Disneyland Paris** resort could keep kids happy for several days (see p.94). Fans of the Astérix comics about ancient Gauls and Romans will enjoy the theme park, **Parc Astérix**, near *Autoroute* A1, open from April to October; tel. (1) 44 62 34 34. **France Miniature** is a 5ha (7.5 acre) relief map of France including model villages, châteaux and monuments to a scale of 1:30 (RER train to St-Quentin-en-Yvelines, then bus; open daily, 15 March-15 November).

Children may not feel enthusiastic at the prospect of long formal meals, but many restaurants offer a short, economical and often very attractive *Menu Enfants* (children's menu). Otherwise, there is a profusion of fast food places, ice cream stands and countless other temptations.

*T*here's plenty of fun on offer besides the obvious attractions for children in Paris.

Eating Out

Dining out is one of the greatest pleasures of Paris. Indeed, for some visitors it's the main objective of their visit. If you have a particular restaurant in mind it's as well to reserve (far ahead for the famous names). Otherwise, finding a place to eat is part of the enjoyment. In areas where they are concentrated, you can take a look at a

selection, sharpening your appetite while you stroll around. Restaurants are obliged to display priced menus outside, so you can compare them, including the day's specials (*plats du jour*). One of the best recommendations is the sight of a crowd inside, especially if it's local people (conversely, note that such places may be empty early in the evening). If there's too long a wait for a table, make a reservation for some other day. (see RECOMMENDED RESTAURANTS, p.74)

Where to Look

No part of Paris is lacking in places to eat, but some areas offer an especially wide range.

On the Left Bank, try between Boulevard Saint-Germain and Pont-Neuf, around Rue Saint-Séverin, in the Rue Mouffetard and its extension, Rue Descartes, and in the area behind Gare Montparnasse.

On the Right Bank, start by looking around Les Halles and the Centre Pompidou, Place de la Bastille and the Marais – including the Jewish quarter.

Further to the west, between Place de l'Opéra and Boulevard Haussmann, to the north of Champs-Elysées and also near Avenue Wagram, north of Place des Ternes.

From mid-July to the end of August, many restaurant owners close up and go off on holiday, reducing the choice.

Menus

A boon to everyone on a budget is the fixed price *table d'hôte* (or *menu fixe*, *prix fixe* or just *menu* – remember, the French word for menu is not *menu* but *carte*). The word *formule* similarly means an all-inclusive special deal. There's frequently the option of starter + main course *or* main course + dessert (or cheese). A drink may be included in the price – either a small carafe of wine, a beer, soft drink or mineral water. In this case you may see the letters b.c. (*boisson comprise*) or v.c. (*vin compris*).

Competition has done wonders in recent years and, in general, you get what you pay for, so a 69F *formule* will be

Don't even try to resist the miniature masterpieces created by the Paris pastry chefs.

simple and the portions probably quite small. If you are on a tight budget, watch out for high-priced extras – apéritifs or coffee – which can add up to as much again as the basic meal. Never order anything without knowing the price.

Tax and service charge are included, signified by t.s.c., s.t.c., or s.c. (*service compris*) at the foot of the menu. A few waiters, if they think they are dealing with somebody new to France, may try to suggest **107** otherwise. If you pay by credit card, the 'extras' line and the total may be left open for you to write in a tip. There is no obligation to do so.

Restaurants must provide a designated non-smoking area. If they don't, they are deemed to be entirely non-smoking.

The Options

At traditional, rather formal **restaurants**, with their own style and speciality dishes, you will be expected to reserve a table, dress up to a degree and spend most of an evening. But there are many other possibilities (although the boundaries between them are blurred). A **bistro** is likely to be small, informal and family-run, and might have lace curtains, tiled floors, wood panelling and red check tablecloths. A modern version may go in for vivid colours, high-tech lighting and strange furniture. Wine comes by the carafe, plus a few bottles, perhaps listed on the back of the single-page menu. A

Economy Measures

- Find a tasty-sounding *formule* or *menu* and avoid any extras.
- Remember, restaurants cost less at lunch-time and might come within your budget.
- Try the ethnic restaurants, and unfashionable parts of Paris – like the east and northeast.
- Buy sandwiches, filled lengths of French bread, from bakeries and grocery stores – prices get inflated at sandwich bars near to tourist sights. Better still, pick up ingredients for a picnic at one of the mini-supermarkets (such as the Félix Potin chain), and look for a bench in a park or beside the Seine.
- Fast food is all over the city, including the usual international names. A big step up in quality but still budget-priced are local chains such as Hippopotamus and Bistro Romain.

bistro à vin (wine bar) makes more of its wines and less of its food, which may be bread and cheese, sausages, quiches. A **pub** in Paris can be facsimile British or Irish, or the local version, usually with a range of beers and hot meals too. Beer comes bottled or draft (*pression*), which costs less. A *demi* is 50cl, less than a pint.

A ***brasserie*** combines the functions of bar, café and restaurant and keeps long hours: some never close at all. They are simply furnished, brightly lit, and can be huge. You can order anything from a drink to a snack or full dinner.

A ***café*** sells more than just coffee: you can have a beer, apéritif, soft drink or snack, even a hot dish of the day (*plat du jour*). You pay more sitting at a table than at the stand-up counter – a cup of coffee could cost twice as much, but you can linger over it for hours. Coffee, incidentally, is *un express*, a small black coffee, unless you specify otherwise (*au lait* is with hot milk).

Many of the older generation in Paris like to meet at a

Neighbourhood cafés can serve as bar, club, snack bar and centre for gossip – all in one.

salon de thé, for a pastry or slice of fruit tart and a cup of tea in the afternoon. Some salons will serve a light lunch too.

Despite this broad choice of eating places, **vegetarians** have a tough time. The tourist office's extensive list includes only three vegetarian restaurants. In practice, it's easy to avoid meat, with plenty of salads, fish, cheese and egg-based dishes, and restaurant chains as well as some chefs are starting to list vegetarian choices.

109

Riches of the Regions

Every part of France proclaims the superiority of its cooking. Paris, with no distinctive cuisine of its own, is a showcase for them all.

Burgundy produces a great beef stew, *bœuf bourguignon*, beef simmered in red wine with mushrooms, small white onions and a little bacon. Its Bresse poultry is considered France's finest and the Charolais beef provides the most tender steaks.

Lyon is renowned for its pork, game, vegetables and fruit. Onion soup (*soupe à l'oignon*) is a local invention; and *à la lyonnaise* generally means sautéed with onions. Dishes include (for starters), *cœurs d'artichaut* (artichoke hearts), or *gratin de queues d'écrevisses* (baked crayfish tails).

Alsace is next to Germany, and does some similar dishes – smoked pork, liver dumplings and *choucroute* (suaerkraut, or pickled cabbage) – but, the French would argue, better!

Brittany is celebrated for its shellfish, served unadorned on a bed of crushed ice and seaweed, as a *plateau de fruits de mer*. It will often include raw oysters, and steamed mussels, clams, scallops, prawns and whelks.

Normandy is famous for its dairy farms. Cream and butter are staples of the cuisine, while the local apples (*reinettes*) turn up with flambéed partridge (*perdreau flambé aux reinettes*) and in *poulet au Calvados* (chicken with apple-brandy sauce). Besides Camembert cheese, sample the stronger Livarot or Pont-l'Evêque.

Bordeaux gave its name to *bordelaise* sauce, made with white or red wine, shallots and beef marrow, served variously with entrecôte steaks, cep mushrooms or lamprey eels (*lamproies*).

Provence makes the most of its garlic, olives, tomatoes and the country's most fragrant herbs. Spicy *tapenade*, an olive and anchovy paste, is delicious on toast. *Daube de bœuf* is beef stew with tomatoes and olives. The celebrated *bouillabaisse* soup should contain half a dozen or more sorts of fish and shellfish – a meal in itself.

The southwestern regions of **Gascony** and **Périgord** are famous for *foie gras* (goose liver), and for *confit d'oie* and *confit de canard*, rich goose and duck preserves, traditionally kept for winter feasting.

Food Fashions

What do restaurants mean by the labels they give to their styles of cooking? By far the most complicated and calorific is *haute cuisine*. Also known as *grande cuisine*, it uses plenty of cream, butter, wine and expensive ingredients such as truffles in its characteristic rich sauces. Worries about cholesterol and the cost of labour have made it a rarity.

Cuisine bourgeoise, or traditional home cooking transferred to the restaurant setting, has become quite the fashion. The *coq au vin*, *blanquette de veau* or other stand-bys might be just like grandmother used to make, or adapted according to the whim of the chef.

Nouvelle cuisine was a reaction to the excesses of traditional *haute cuisine*, making use of fresh ingredients, lightly cooked and artistically presented. Some chefs went too far, serving tiny portions and bizarre combinations, turning it into a bad joke. That period is largely over, but the better ideas have survived. To escape the negative image, the vague term *cuisine gastronomique* is used instead, to describe creative cooking in the modern manner – colourful and inventive without being too fussy. French chefs have been travelling a lot in recent years, picking up ideas from India, China, Thailand and Japan. There's no doubt about it: the food in Paris is better than ever.

Y ou can eat simply and well, without spending a fortune – try the set menu at a brasserie.

Ethnic Variations

Parisians have taken to ethnic restaurants in a big way, and nowadays you can find almost as many variations as nations at the UN. Chinese restaurants were among the first – many of them are now luxurious establishments around the Champs-Elysées area and Les Halles. Vietnamese, Laotian and Cambodian food has caught on, with dozens of places to be found in the Latin Quarter and the 13th *arrondissement*, behind the Place d'Italie, home to numerous immigrants from southeast Asia. Their cuisine features distinctive touches of mint, coriander, lemon-grass (*citronelle*) and ginger, and a great variety of seafood. Thai restaurants have multiplied in Paris, as they have in almost every western capital. More and more Japanese restaurants also appear each year, with plenty of tourists from Japan to encourage a certain degree of authenticity.

Greek, Turkish and Lebanese restaurants are scattered along the Left Bank, notably near Rue Saint-Séverin. The shabby northeastern suburb of Belleville, home to a sizeable Algerian and Moroccan community, has the most authentic North African cooking. Italian restaurants may be found virtually everywhere. Indian food is also making great headway, going beyond simple curries and tandoori to the wonderful subtleties of the Mughal and Kashmiri cuisines.

Savoury and sweet Arabic specialities are ideal for a picnic break between sightseeing.

Wines

French wine lists rarely mention anything that isn't French. The great names of Bordeaux and Burgundy and of course Champagne are still the ones the rest of the world wants to beat, but there's a host of other regional wines too, much more reasonably priced.

Usually only the top flight restaurants have wine waiters (*sommeliers*) who know much about the subject. They'll be happy if you seek their help, and probably unruffled if you don't. Elsewhere, the regular waiter or waitress will take your wine order. There is seldom any point in asking their advice. Mark-ups are generally high (three to four times that of wine store prices) so unless you see a known favourite, it's just as well to go for a carafe (*pichet*) of the house wine (*vin de la maison*). Most French people will be doing the same. In summer, don't be surprised if the red wine comes chilled (*frais*). It's the custom, and an easy one to get used to.

To Help You Order ...

Do you have a table?
I would like (a/an/some) ...

Avez-vous une table?
J'aimerais ...

beer	**une bière**	mineral water	**de l'eau minérale**
butter	**du beurre**		
bread	**du pain**	sparkling/ still	**gazeuse/ non gazeuse**
cheese	**du fromage**		
chips (fries)	**des frites**	pepper	**du poivre**
coffee	**un café**	salad	**une salade**
dessert	**un dessert**	salt	**du sel**
fish	**du poisson**	seafood	**fruits de mer**
glass	**un verre**	soup	**de la soupe**
meat	**de la viande**	sugar	**du sucre**
menu	**la carte**	tea	**du thé**
milk	**du lait**	wine	**du vin**

113

... and Read the Menu

agneau	lamb	**jambon**	ham
asperges	asparagus	**langouste**	rock lobster
bar	sea bass	**lapin**	rabbit
boeuf	beef	**moules**	mussels
caille	quail	**nouilles**	noodles
canard	duck	**oignons**	onions
caneton	duckling	**petits pois**	peas
cerises	cherries	**pintade**	guinea fowl
champignons	mushrooms	**poire**	pear
charcuterie	cold cooked meats/sausage	**poireaux**	leeks
		pomme	apple
chou	cabbage	**pomme de terre**	potato
choufleur	cauliflower		
crevettes roses/grises	prawns/ shrimps	**porc**	pork
		poulet	chicken
crudités	raw vegetables	**raisins**	grapes
daurade	sea bream	**ris de veau**	calf's sweetbreads
échalotes	shallots		
épinards	spinach	**riz**	rice
farci	stuffed	**rognon**	kidney
foie	liver	**rouget**	red mullet
fraises	strawberries	**saucisse**	sausage
framboises	raspberries	**saumon**	salmon
haricots verts	green beans	**thon**	tuna
homard	lobster	**truite**	trout
huitres	oysters	**veau**	veal

So how would you like your steak?

very rare	**bleu**	medium	**à point**
rare	**saignant**	well done	**bien cuit**
medium-rare	**rose**		

BLUEPRINT
for a
Perfect Trip

An A–Z Summary of Practical Information

A

ACCOMMODATION (see also RECOMMENDED HOTELS starting on p.66, YOUTH HOSTELS on p.139 and CAMPING on p.118)

Paris has hotels to suit every taste and budget. The city is a popular destination all year round, so booking in advance is recommended. See p.117 for information about making reservations at the airport. During big commercial fairs (*salons*), rooms are hard to find.

Hotels are officially classified into five categories; a complete booklet is available from the Paris Tourist Information Office (see p.133). Rates naturally depend on the hotel's amenities and location, and are posted visibly at reception desks.

Few but the most expensive hotels have air-conditioning. In those without it, you will want to have the windows open in summer, so ask for a room that doesn't face a noisy street.

For a long stay you might consider renting. Travel sections of national newspapers carry advertisements and, on the spot, *Le Figaro* and the *International Herald Tribune* list accommodation for rent.

Do you have a single/double room for tonight?	**Avez-vous une chambre pour une/deux personnes pour cette nuit?**
What's the rate per night?	**Quel est le prix pour une nuit?**

AIRPORTS (*aéroport*)

Paris has two main airports. Roissy-Charles-de-Gaulle is about 25km (15 miles) northeast of the city and has two terminals, CDG 1 for most international flights; CDG 2 mainly for Air France flights.

Orly (for most domestic and many European flights) is about 15km (9 miles) to the south, with two buildings, Orly-Sud and Orly-Ouest. Both airports have exchange facilities, good restaurants, snack-bars, post offices and duty-free shops.

Regular **buses** link the two main airports with Paris and each other, and run frequently from about 6am to 11pm. The city terminals (*aérogare*) for Charles-de-Gaulle airport are at Porte Maillot, near l'Etoile, and at Opéra (Rue Scribe); you can also board the bus at the Arc de Triomphe (Avenue Carnot). *Roissybus* from Opéra takes about 45 minutes. Orly is served by buses to the Invalides city terminal (40 minutes journey) and by the *Orlybus* (every 15 minutes to/from Denfert-Rochereau RER station, taking about 30 minutes).

Taxis are plentiful, but more expensive from the airport (see p.135).

RER trains run every 15 minutes from about 5.30am to 11.30pm between Charles-de-Gaulle airport and Gare du Nord; the trip takes 35-40 minutes. Orly is served by *Orlyval* trains which connect with RER line B (opposite platform) to central Paris; alternatively, use RER Line C which runs to the Gare d'Austerlitz, Saint-Michel and Musée d'Orsay stations: journey time is about 35 minutes.

Hotel reservations can be made in the airport arrival halls. At CDG 1 go to Porte 36, where a desk is open from 7.30am to 11pm. (A deposit of 12% is required, which will be deducted from the bill.) Alternatively, the electronic notice board next to the desk enables you to contact (free of charge) a wide range of hotels throughout the city. CDG 2 has similar amenities. For further general information, call the Renseignements Généraux service on (1) 48 62 22 80 (Charles-de-Gaulle) or (1) 49 75 15 15 (Orly). Most staff speak English.

B

BICYCLE HIRE (RENTAL) (*location de bicyclettes*)
You can hire bikes by the day or week, for example at: Paris-Vélo, 2 Rue du Fer à Moulin, 75005; tel.(1) 43 37 59 22, and Mountain Bike Trip, 6 Place Etienne Pernet, 75015; tel.(1) 48 42 57 87.

These and other companies also run guided tours by bicycle: tourist information offices can supply a longer list. In the Bois de Boulogne, old-fashioned bikes are available by the hour near the Jardin d'Acclimatation (see p.63). You'll be asked for an identity document or a large deposit.

C

CAMPING

The only site reasonably close to the centre of Paris is in the Bois de Boulogne, beside the Seine. It gets crowded in summer. A number of other sites are in striking distance, at Champigny-sur-Marne, Torcy and St-Quentin-en-Yvelines, all on the RER suburban train network.

CAR HIRE (RENTAL) (*location de voitures*)

Local firms may offer lower prices than international companies, but the latter will often let you return the car at any branch in the country at no extra cost. Ask about seasonal and other special deals.

To hire a car, you must show your driving licence (held for at least a year) and passport. You also need a major credit card, or a large deposit will be required. The minimum age for hiring cars ranges from 20 to 23, and a maximum of 65 is imposed by some companies. Third-party insurance is compulsory, but full cover is recommended.

Yellow Pages (*Pages Jaunes*) list the companies, under *Location de voitures*.

I'd like to hire a car now/tomorrow.	**Je voudrais louer une voiture tout de suite/demain.**
for one day/a week	**pour une journée/une semaine**

CLIMATE and CLOTHING

Paris enjoys a mild continental climate. Extremes of heat or cold are rare, although in July and August daytime temperatures often exceed 30°C (86°F). In most respects, the best seasons for a visit are spring and autumn, though winter is perfectly bearable.

The chart below is for average monthly temperatures (daily high).

	J	F	M	A	M	J	J	A	S	O	N	D
temperature °C	8	7	10	16	17	23	25	26	21	17	12	8
temperature °F	46	45	50	61	63	73	77	79	70	63	54	46

Clothing. In common with most capitals, Paris is a lot less formal than it used to be. More formal restaurants still expect men to wear a jacket and tie. In the heat of midsummer you will want to have light cotton clothing that you can wash and hang up to dry overnight. A raincoat is useful in winter, and an umbrella at any time.

COMMUNICATIONS

Post Offices (*poste*). These display a stylized blue bird and the sign *La Poste*. They are usually open from 8am to 7pm Monday to Friday and 8am-noon on Saturday. The city's main post office at 52 Rue du Louvre is open 24 hours a day, every day. The post office at 71, Avenue des Champs-Elysée is open until 10pm on weekdays, and opens on Sundays and public holidays (10am-noon, 2-8pm).

As well as the usual mail services, you can make phone calls, buy *télécartes* (phone cards) and send faxes.

Letters may be delivered within hours in the Paris district by sending them *postexpress* from the post office. Another quick system for delivering a message is the *message téléphoné*; tel. 36 55.

N.B. While you can theoretically buy stamps (*timbres poste*) at tobacconists (*tabacs*) or souvenir shops, the salespeople are disinclined to sell them unless you purchase something else. You can, however, buy phonecards there (see p.120).

Mail (*courrier*). If you don't know ahead of time where you'll be staying, you can have your mail addressed to you *poste restante* (general delivery) c/o Poste restante, 52 Rue du Louvre, 75001 Paris (open always). You can collect it for a small fee on presentation of your passport. American Express, at 11 Rue Scribe, 75009 Paris, performs the same service.

The **Minitel** computer terminal found in most French homes can be used for everything from making TGV train reservations to booking a theatre ticket, joining a dating service or looking up someone's telephone number or address. Visitors can find one in most post offices: a phonecard is needed to operate it. You may need help from a French person at first although there's nothing very complicated about it. Instructions on screen are in French, but you may find a booklet in English at offices of France Télécom.

Telephones (*téléphone*). Long-distance and international calls can be made from any phone box, but if you need assistance, you can call from post offices or your hotel (you'll usually pay a supplement).

The system is efficient and simple, but most Paris phone boxes only take **phonecards** (*télécartes*). You can buy cards of 50 or 120 units (48F or 96F respectively) at post offices or tobacconists. Don't get caught without one on a Sunday when few places selling them are open. Coin-operated phones consume 50c and 1, 2 and 5F coins.

To make an **international** call, dial 19 followed by the country code, area code (omitting any initial zero) and number. For international inquiries, add 33 between 19 and the code of your chosen country, e.g. 19 33 44 (inquiries for the UK). For inquiries on US or Canadian numbers, dial 11 instead of 1 (i.e. 19 33 11).

For long-distance calls within France, there are no area codes (just dial the 8-digit number), except when telephoning from Paris or its region (Ile-de-France) to the provinces (dial 16 and then the 8-digit number). From the provinces to Paris or the Ile-de-France (dial 16, then 1 followed by the 8-digit number). Paris numbers begin with a 4, Ile de France numbers with 3 or 6. If all else fails, call the operator for help (12).

Faxes. Hotels can send them for you, though the charges can be high. Larger post offices offer fax services.

COMPLAINTS

If you have a complaint, make it on the spot, pleasantly and calmly, and to the correct person. At a hotel or restaurant, ask to speak to the manager (*directeur* or *maître d'hôtel*). In extreme cases only, a police station (*commissariat de police*) may help or, failing that, outside Paris, try the regional administration offices (the *préfecture* or *sous-préfecture*). Ask for the *service du tourisme*.

CRIME (see also LOST PROPERTY on p.126)

Keep items of value and any large amounts of money in hotel safe boxes. Beware of being crowded by street children whose aim is to get their fingers into your pockets or handbags. Never leave a car unlocked. Don't leave anything in view when parked, and if possible remove the radio. Avoid walking alone in dark streets and travelling late on the métro, though the risks are no greater than in most cities.

Any loss or theft should be reported as soon as possible to the nearest police station. A report will help with the insurance claim.

CUSTOMS (*douane*) and ENTRY FORMALITIES

Nationals of EU countries and Switzerland need only a valid passport or identity document to enter France. Nationals from Canada, New Zealand and the USA require passports whilst Australian and South African nationals must obtain a visa. For the latest information on entry requirements, contact the French embassy in your country.

As France belongs to the European Union (EU), free exchange of non-duty-free goods for personal use is permitted between France and the UK and Eire. However, duty-free items are still subject to restrictions: again, check before you go.

For residents of non-EU countries, restrictions when going home are as follows: **Australia**: 250 cigarettes **or** 250g of tobacco; 1 litre alcohol; **Canada**: 200 cigarettes **and** 50 cigars **and** 400g tobacco; 4.5l wine or beer **and** 1.1 litre spirits: **South Africa**: 400 cigarettes **and** 50 cigars **and** 250g tobacco; 2l wine **and** 1 litre spirits; **USA**: 200 cigarettes **and** 100 cigars **or** a 'reasonable amount' of tobacco; 1 litre wine or spirits.

Currency restrictions. There's no limit on the amount of local or foreign currencies or traveller's cheques that can be brought into France, but amounts in banknotes exceeding 50,000 French francs (or equivalent) should be declared if you intend to export them.

DRIVING IN FRANCE

To take a car into France, you will need: a valid driving licence; car registration papers; insurance cover (the green card is no longer obligatory but comprehensive cover is advisable); a red warning triangle and a set of spare bulbs are strongly recommended.

The minimum driving age is 18. Drivers and front- and back-seat passengers are required by law to wear seat belts. Children under 10 may not travel in the front (unless the car has no back seat). Driving on a foreign provisional licence is not permitted.

Driving regulations. As elsewhere on the continent, drive on the right, overtake (pass) on the left. At roundabouts (traffic circles), vehicles already in the roundabout have right of way. Otherwise, in built-up areas, give priority to vehicles coming from the right. In other areas, the more important of the two roads (indicated by a yellow diamond) has right of way. The use of car horns in built-up areas is allowed only as a warning. At night, lights should be used for this purpose. Don't drink and drive: random breath tests are frequent and the alcohol limit is very low (corresponding to one **small** drink).

Speed limits. The limit is 50km/h (31mph) in built-up areas and 80 km/h (50mph) on the *périphérique* ring road. Elsewhere it is 90km/h (55mph); 110km/h (70mph) on dual carriageways; 130km/h (around 80mph) on *autoroutes* (toll motorways). Note: when roads are wet, limits are reduced by 10km/h (6mph), and by 20km/h (12mph) on motorways. In fog, the limit is 50km/h (31mph). Police speed traps are common, and you can be fined heavily, on the spot, for offences.

Road conditions. Driving in Paris can be an exciting experience. Thanks to Haussmann's broad avenues and the Seine-side *voie express*, traffic generally sweeps through the capital at a tolerable speed – but you can't rely on it and horrendous jams can form. The ring road (*périphérique*) round Paris tends to get clogged at rush hours. Note that motorways (*autoroutes*) outside Paris are expensive.

For advance information on traffic conditions, radio France-Inter's *Inter-Route* service operates 24 hours a day. Most of the time, English-speaking staff will be there to help you; tel. (1) 48 94 33 33.

Parking (*stationnement*). This is a nightmare (as in most capitals), which is why it's better to walk, use the métro or take a bus. In the centre most street parking is metered and the spaces marked '*Payant*'. You buy a ticket at a nearby machine and display it inside the car. Never park in bus lanes, express lanes or anywhere that isn't clearly permitted or your car may be towed away to an obscure pound, only to be retrieved at great expense.

Breakdowns. It's wise to take out an international breakdown insurance before leaving home. Always ask for an estimate before authorizing repairs, and expect to pay TVA (value-added tax) on top of the cost. Two companies which offer 24-hour breakdown service are Automobile Club Secours, tel. (1) 05 05 05 24 (toll-free) and SOS Dépannage, tel. (1) 47 07 99 99.

Fuel and oil (*essence*; *huile*). Fuel is available as super (98 octane), normal (90 octane), lead-free (*sans plomb* – 98 or 95 octane) and diesel (gas-oil). Note that many garages are shut on Sundays. Avoid buying fuel on motorways: try to get to a supermarket to fill up – there can be as much as a 15% difference in price.

Road signs. Most signs are the standard pictographs used throughout Europe, but you may encounter these written signs as well:

Déviation	Diversion (detour)
Péage	Toll
Priorité à droite	Yield to traffic from right
Vous n'avez pas la priorité	Give way
Ralentir	Slow down
Serrez à droite/à gauche	Keep right/left
Sens unique	One way
Rappel	Restriction continues (a reminder)

driving licence	**permis de conduire**
car registration papers	**carte grise**
Fill the tank, please.	**Le plein, s'il vous plaît.**
My car has broken down.	**Ma voiture est en panne.**
There's been an accident.	**Il y a eu un accident.**

E

ELECTRIC CURRENT

You'll need an adaptor for most British and US plugs: French sockets have round holes. Supplies are 220 volt, and US equipment will need a transformer. Shaver outlets are generally dual voltage.

EMBASSIES and CONSULATES

For any major problem, such as loss of a passport or all your money, a serious accident or trouble with the police, contact your consulate or embassy.

Australia embassy and consulate: 4 Rue Jean-Rey, 75015 Paris; tel. (1) 40 59 33 00; fax (1) 40 59 33 10.

Canada embassy: 35 Avenue Montaigne, 75008 Paris; tel. (1) 44 43 29 16; fax (1) 44 43 29 99.

Republic of Ireland embassy: 12 Avenue Foch (enter from 4 Rue Rude), 75016 Paris; tel. (1) 45 00 20 87; fax (1) 45 00 84 17.

New Zealand embassy: 7 ter Rue Léonardo-da-Vinci, 75116 Paris; tel. (1) 45 00 24 11; fax (1) 45 01 26 39.

South Africa consulate: 59 Quai d'Orsay, 75443 Paris Cedex 07; tel. (1) 45 55 92 37; fax (1) 47 53 99 70.

United Kingdom embassy: 35 Rue du Faubourg-Saint-Honoré, 75008 Paris; tel. (1) 42 66 91 42; consulate: 16, Rue d'Anjou, 75008 Paris; tel. (1) 42 66 06 68; fax (1) 40 76 02 87.

USA embassy: 2 Avenue Gabriel, 75008 Paris; tel. (1) 42 96 12 02. Consulate: 2 Rue St Florentin, 75001 Paris (same tel.); fax (1) 42 66 05 33/42 66 97 83.

EMERGENCIES *(urgence)*

For 24hr assistance anywhere in France dial:

Police *(police secours)*	17
Fire brigade *(pompiers)*	18
Ambulance (SAMU)	15

Paris has an efficient anti-poison centre: tel. (1) 40 37 04 04. You can get advice for other urgent medical problems by calling SOS Médecins on (1) 47 07 77 77 or the SAMU on (1) 45 67 50 50.

Police!	**Police!**
Fire!	**Au feu!**
Help!	**Au secours!**

ETIQUETTE

Be sure to say *Bonjour, monsieur* or *Bonjour, madame* (or *mademoiselle* to an unmarried woman) to anyone you meet, including staff when you go into a small shop. It is usual to shake hands when introduced, and again on saying goodbye. French friends exchange kisses on alternate cheeks, and not just two, but three, four or more.

Business people dress quite formally, and meetings are punctual and efficient. In contrast, you will not be expected to turn up too promptly for social functions. It is unusual to be invited to private houses: you are more likely to be entertained at a restaurant.

GAY and LESBIAN PARIS

The city has a large and visible gay community: the midsummer Gay Pride festival is a major event. Favourite bars, clubs, cabarets and discos are concentrated in the Les Halles-Marais-Bastille strip.

GUIDES and TOURS (see also Getting Around on p.22)

Multilingual guides and interpreters can be found through the Office de Tourisme de Paris (see p.133). Their monthly booklet *Paris Sélection* lists telephone contacts.

L

LANGUAGE (see also the USEFUL EXPRESSIONS on the cover)

Even if your French isn't perfect, don't feel inhibited: it's better to make an effort. Never assume that people will speak English.

The Berlitz FRENCH PHRASE BOOK AND DICTIONARY covers almost all the situations you're likely to encounter in your travels; it's also available as part of the Berlitz FRENCH CASSETTE PACK. In addition, the Berlitz FRENCH-ENGLISH/ENGLISH-FRENCH POCKET DICTIONARY contains a glossary of 12,500 terms, plus a menu-reader supplement.

LOST PROPERTY (objets trouvés)

If loss or suspected theft occurs in your hotel, check first at the desk. They may suggest that you report the loss to the local police station (*commissariat*). Restaurant and hotel personnel will look after objects left behind; they turn over valuables to the police.

Lost property may turn up at the Bureau des Objets Trouvés, 36 Rue des Morillons, 75015 Paris. If you have lost a passport, check first with your embassy, as the Bureau would transfer it there.

| I have lost my | **J'ai perdu mon** |
| wallet/handbag/passport. | **portefeuille/sac/passeport.** |

MEDIA

Radio and TV. You'll find Paris FM radio stations specializing in classical music, rock and pop (their own, which tends not to travel outside France). The BBC World Service can be heard on medium and short-wave, BBC Radio 4 on long-wave and The Voice of America on short-wave.

The regular French TV channels are notably bland, but most hotels have a range of cable services: CNN, Sky, BBC, and programmes from Germany, Japan, even Saudi Arabia, as well as French subscription channels (some carrying late-night explicit sex).

Newspapers and Magazines (*journal*; *revue/magazine*). As well as the French press, a wide range of dailies, weeklies and monthlies is available in English and other languages. You'll find them in kiosks and *maisons de la Presse*. *Pariscope* and *L'Officiel des Spectacles* are weekly guides to what's on. The free monthly *Paris Sélection* (available from tourist offices) lists concerts, festivals and shows.

MEDICAL CARE (see also EMERGENCIES on p.125)

To put your mind at rest, make sure your health insurance policy covers any illness or accident while on holiday.

Visitors from EU countries with corresponding health insurance facilities are entitled to medical and hospital treatment under the French social security system. Before leaving home, find out about the appropriate forms and formalities.

Paris has excellent doctors, surgeons and medical facilities. Most bigger hotels or the consulates have a list of English-speaking doctors and dentists. Doctors who belong to the French social security system (*médecins conventionnés*) charge the minimum.

Two private hospitals serve the Anglo-American community: the American Hospital of Paris, 63, Bd. Victor-Hugo, 92202 Neuilly, tel. (1) 46 41 25 25; and the Hôpital Franco-Britannique, 3 Rue Barbès, 92300 Levallois-Perret, tel. (1) 46 39 22 22.

Chemist shops (*pharmacies*) are easily identified by the green cross they display. They are helpful in dealing with minor ailments and can recommend a nurse (*infirmière*) if you need injections or special care. There's always a chemist on night-duty (*service de garde*) and its name and address is displayed in the window of other pharmacies. The Pharmacie Dhery, 84 Ave. des Champs-Elysées, tel. (1) 45 62 02 41, is open 24 hours a day (métro: George V).

MONEY MATTERS

Currency. The French franc (abbreviated F, Fr or FF) is divided into 100 centimes (c or ct). Coins (*pièces*) come in 5, 10, 20, 50 centimes (marked ½F); 1, 2, 5, 10 and 20F. Banknotes (*billets*) come in 20, 50, 100, 200 and 500F. For currency restrictions, see p.121.

Banks and currency exchange offices (*banque*; *bureau de change*) (see also OPENING HOURS on p.129). Always take your passport when you go to change money or traveller's cheques. Your hotel may also offer an exchange service, though at a less favourable exchange rate. The same applies to foreign currency or traveller's cheques changed in stores, boutiques, tourist offices or restaurants.

I want to change some pounds/dollars.	**Je voudrais changer des livres sterling/des dollars.**

Credit cards are widely accepted in hotels, restaurants, shops and petrol (gas) stations. You may be able to use your card to withdraw cash from automatic teller machines (*DAB, distributeurs automatiques de billets*), but some machines only respond to French-issued 'smart' cards. If your card is rejected by the machine, you can go to a bank exchange counter to obtain cash with it. Visa cardholders can call freephone 05 90 82 81 (no prefix) for assistance.

Traveller's cheques (with identification) and **Eurocheques** (with encashment card) are widely accepted.

Sales tax. A value-added tax (TVA) is imposed on almost all goods and services, and is usually included in the price. In hotels and restaurants, this is on top of a service charge (also included).

Visitors from non-EU countries can have the TVA refunded on major purchases of goods for export (see p.97).

Do you accept traveller's cheques/this credit card?	**Acceptez-vous les chèques de voyage/cette carte de crédit?**

Planning your Budget

The following prices in French francs should give you an idea of costs during a visit to Paris. However, they must be regarded as approximate; inflation in France, as elsewhere, pushes prices up.

Airport transfer. Bus to Orly 30F, to Charles-de-Gaulle 48F; train (second class) to Orly 25F, to Charles-de-Gaulle 30F. Taxi to Orly 140F, to Charles-de-Gaulle 220F.

128 **Bicycle hire**. 44/55F per day, plus 1,500-2,000F refundable deposit.

Car hire (international company). Renault Clio: 250F per day, 4F per km, 1,900F per week with unlimited mileage. Renault Safrane: 500F per day, 7F per km, 4,000F per week with unlimited mileage. Tax and insurance included.

Entertainment. *Discothèque* (admission and first drink) 80-150F; nightclub with dinner and floor show 400-800F; cinema 40-50F.

Guides. 800F for a half-day.

Hotels (double room with bath). ****Luxe 2,200F+; **** 1,500-2,200F; *** 900-1,500F; ** 450-900F; * 200-450F.

Meals and drinks. Continental breakfast in hotel 40-150F; in café 30-60F. Lunch 90-200F, dinner 200-350F and upwards, fast food meal 25-40F, coffee 8-12F, soft drink 10-20F, beer 20-40F, small carafe of wine 20-30F, bottle of wine 100F and up, cocktail 40-90F.

Métro (tickets also valid on buses). 7F; 10 tickets (*carnet*) 44F; weekly ticket (city, near suburbs, Monday to Sunday) 63F; monthly 219F. 'Paris Visite' ticket 95F for three days, 150F for five days.

Sightseeing. Boats: adults 48F, children 20F. Monuments and museums: 25-50F (children less, or free). Museum Pass: (see p.88) 70F for one day, 140F for three, 200F for five days.

Taxis start at 12F (an extra 5F is charged at train stations and air terminals), plus about 3.50F per kilometre. Night rates are higher.

OPENING HOURS (*heures d'ouverture*) (see also PUBLIC HOLIDAYS on p.131)

Avoid using lunch hours for 'administrative' tasks: although the long Parisian lunch is becoming a distant memory, businesses and smaller shops may close for an hour or so, between 12 and 2.30pm.

Banks tend to open 9am-5pm on weekdays (many closing for lunch from 12 to 2pm) and close either on Saturdays or Mondays. All banks close on major national holidays and most close early on the day before a public holiday.

Main **post offices** are open 8am-7pm on weekdays and 8am-noon on Saturdays. Smaller post offices close for lunch from 12 to 2 or 2.30pm, and close at 5 or 6pm.

Grocers, bakeries, tobacconists, food shops are open from 7 or 8am to 7pm (or later, sometimes up to midnight), Monday-Saturday. Food shops are often open on Sunday morning. Small shops usually shut at lunch-time, 12.30-2pm.

Other shops, department stores, boutiques are open from 9, 9.30 or 10am to 6.30 or 7pm (sometimes later in summer), Tuesday to Saturday. They are closed Monday morning or all day Monday.

Museums are open 10am-5, 5.30 or 6pm (variable). Some, including the Louvre, are closed on Tuesdays: others close on Mondays. Major national monuments including the Arc de Triomphe, Panthéon and Sainte-Chapelle are open daily, except certain public holidays. (See also Major Museums on p.81 and Paris Highlights on p.35.)

P

PHOTOGRAPHY and VIDEO

For detailed information on how to get the most out of your holiday photographs, purchase a copy of the Berlitz-Nikon GUIDE TO TRAVEL PHOTOGRAPHY (available in the UK only).

All types of blank video tape are available, but note that pre-recorded cassettes sold in France are not compatible with UK or US systems. Those specifically made as travel souvenirs will be appropriately marked.

I'd like a film for this camera	**J'aimerais un film pour cet appareil.**
a colour-slide film	**un film de diapositives**
How long will it take to develop this film?	**Combien de temps faut-il pour développer ce film?**
130 May I take a picture?	**Puis-je prendre une photo?**

POLICE (see also EMERGENCIES on p.125)

The blue-uniformed police who keep law and order and direct traffic are as a general rule most courteous and helpful to visitors. The CRS (*Compagnies républicaines de sécurité*) are the tough guys, seen wielding batons and quelling demonstrations that have got out of hand. Outside Paris and other main cities, the *gendarmes*, in blue trousers and black jackets with white belts, are responsible for traffic and crime investigation.

If you need to call for police help, dial **17** (anywhere in France).

Where's the nearest police station?	**Où est le commissariat de police le plus proche?**

PUBLIC HOLIDAYS (*jours fériés*)

Public offices, banks and most shops close on public holidays, though you'll find the odd corner shop open. If one of these days falls on a Tuesday or Thursday, many French people take the Monday or Friday off as well for a long weekend (this doesn't usually curtail activity in shops or businesses, however).

1 January	*Jour de l'An*	New Year's Day
1 May	*Fête du Travail*	Labour Day
8 May	*Fête de la Victoire*	Victory Day (1945)
14 July	*Fête nationale*	Bastille Day
15 August	*Assomption*	Assumption
1 November	*Toussaint*	All Saints' Day
11 November	*Armistice*	Armistice Day (1918)
25 December	*Noël*	Christmas Day
Movable dates:	*Lundi de Pâques*	Easter Monday
	Ascension	Ascension
	Lundi de Pentecôte	Whit Monday

Are you open tomorrow?	**Est-ce que vous ouvrez demain?**

RELIGION

These days, a live-and-let-live atmosphere towards religion prevails, with only occasional arguments about educational funding.

Immigration has brought sizeable Jewish and Muslim communities to Paris, as well as many other smaller groups. The Yellow Pages (*Les Pages Jaunes*), found in most hotel rooms and at all hotel desks, list places of worship of every persuasion.

TIME DIFFERENCES

France keeps to Central European Time (GMT + 1hr). In summer clocks are put one hour ahead (GMT + 2hrs), coming into force from late March to end September. With this in mind, the following chart gives **summer** time differences.

New York	London	**Paris**	Sydney	Auckland
6am	11am	**noon**	8pm	10pm

What time is it? **Quelle heure est-il?**

TIPPING

A little tip can go a long way in Paris. Service is *included* in restaurant bills (though a few waiters may try to persuade you otherwise). Increasingly, tips are given only for an appreciated extra service.

Hotel porter, per bag	5F
Hotel maid, per week	50-100F
Lavatory attendant	4F
Cinema usher(ette)	5F
Taxi driver	10-15%
Tour guide	10%

TOILETS/RESTROOMS (*toilettes*)

Public toilets come in the form of curved booths and are found all over Paris. They cost 2F to use and clean themselves after the user has left. Bars and cafés also have facilities – if you are not a customer, leave two or three francs in the dish provided, or at the bar.

TOURIST INFORMATION OFFICES (*office de tourisme*)

Before going to Paris you can obtain a lot of up-to-date information from the French National Tourist Office in your country. In Paris, you'll find the **Office de Tourisme de Paris** (Visitors Bureau) at 127 Avenue des Champs-Elysées, 75008 Paris; tel. (1) 49 52 53 54; fax (1) 49 52 53 00. Staff will be able to help you with information and booking accommodation; the office is open 9am-8pm every day except 1 May. You can change money there, and buy phonecards and the Museum Pass. Other branches are located in major stations, the Eiffel Tower (May to September) and airport terminals.

For a selection of weekly events in English, call (1) 49 52 53 56. For information on the region surrounding Paris, contact the CRT Ile de France, 26, Avenue de l'Opéra, 75015 Paris; tel. (1) 42 60 28 62.

There are French National Tourist Offices in these countries:

Australia: Kindersley House, 33 Bligh Street, Sydney, NSW 2000; tel. (2) 231 5244.

Canada: 1981 Avenue McGill College, Suite 490, Esso Tower, Montreal, Que. H3A 2W9; tel. (514) 288 4264; 1, Dundas St. West, Suite 2405, Box 8, Toronto, Ont. M5G 1Z3; tel. (416) 593 4717.

South Africa: Carlton Centre, 10th Floor, P.O. Box 1081, Johannesburg 2000; tel. (11) 331 9252.

UK: 178 Piccadilly, London W1V 0AL; tel. (0891) 244 123; fax (0171) 493 6594.

USA: 610 Fifth Avenue, New York, NY 10020; tel. (212) 757 1125.; 645 North Michigan Avenue, Suite 630, Chicago, Illinois 60611; tel. (312) 337 6301; 9401 Wilshire Boulevard, Beverly Hills, CA 90212; tel. (213) 272 2661; 1 Hallidie Plaza, San Francisco, CA 94102; tel. (415) 986 4174; World Trade Center, N103, 2050 Stemmons Freeway, P.O. Box 58610, Dallas, Texas 75258; tel. (214) 742 7011.

TRANSPORT

Bus (*autobus*). Bus transport round Paris is efficient though not always fast. Stops are marked by red and yellow signs, with the bus numbers posted, and you'll find bus itineraries displayed under bus shelters. You can obtain a general bus route plan from métro station ticket offices.

Most buses run from 7am to 8.30pm, some till 12.30am. Service is reduced on Sundays and public holidays. Special buses for night-owls, the 'Noctambus', run along ten main routes serving the capital, from 1.30am to 5.30am every hour, with Châtelet as the hub.

Bus journeys may take up one, two or three tickets, depending on the distance. You can buy a ticket as you board, but it's cheaper to buy a book of tickets (*carnet*), from any métro station. (Bus and métro tickets are interchangeable.) You can also buy special one-, three- or five-day tourist passes or the weekly ticket and *carte orange* (see Métro, below). Show these special tickets to the driver as you get on: **don't** put them in the punching machine.

Métro. The Paris *Métropolitain* (*métro* for short) is one of the world's most efficient, fast and convenient underground railway systems. It's also one of the least expensive, and it keeps growing to accommodate passengers' needs. Express lines (**RER**) get you into the centre of Paris from distant suburbs in approximately 15 minutes, with a few stops in between.

You get ten journeys for the price of six by investing in a *carnet* (book) of tickets, also valid for the bus network and for the RER, provided that you stay within Paris and don't go to outer suburbs. A special ticket called ***Paris Visite***, valid for three or five days, allows unlimited travel on bus or métro, and reductions on entrance fees to various attractions. A **day ticket**, *Formule 1*, is valid for métro, RER, buses, suburban trains and airport buses.

For longer stays, the best buy is a **weekly ticket** (*coupon hebdomadaire*): note that validity runs from each Monday to Sunday. Be sure to ask for the *carte orange* to go with it – and have a passport photo ready to stick to the *carte orange*. For prices, see p.129.

Whatever your ticket, remember to collect it after putting it through the machine at the métro entrance gates (although most of the gates won't open until you do).

Métro stations have big, easy-to-read maps. Service starts at 5.30am and finishes at around 1am – it is not recommended to travel alone after about 10.30pm. The RATP (métro organisation) has an information office at 53 ter Quai des Grands Augustins, 75271 Paris cedex. You can call them round the clock on (1) 43 46 14 14.

Train (*train*). The SNCF (French Railways Authority) runs fast, comfortable trains on an efficient network. The high-speed services (TGV – *trains à grande vitesse*) operating on selected routes are excellent, but more expensive than the average train. Seat reservation on TGVs is compulsory, and you have to pay for it.

The main stations in Paris are the Gare du Nord (for the Eurostar to London, and for Belgium and Netherlands), Gare de l'Est (eastern France and Germany), Gare Saint-Lazare (Normandy and Calais), Gare d'Austerlitz (southwestern France and Spain), Gare Montparnasse (western France) and Gare de Lyon (Provence, Switzerland and Italy).

You must get your train ticket punched before boarding, by inserting it in one of the orange machines (called a *machine à composter* or *composteur*) on the way to the platform. If it is not clipped and dated, the ticket collector is entitled to fine you on the train.

Taxi (*taxi*). Convenient and quick, taxis are reasonably priced, though there'll be extras for putting luggage in the boot (trunk) and for pick-up at a station or airport. Also, taxis can refuse to carry more than three passengers.

You'll find taxis cruising around, or at stands all over the city. Ask for a receipt if you need it (*un reçu*). Rates differ according to the zones covered or the time of the day (you'll be charged more between 7pm and 7am, and on Sundays). An average fare between Roissy-Charles-de-Gaulle Airport and Paris centre might be 220F by day, 280F at night. If you have any problems with a driver, you can register a complaint with the Service des Taxis, 36 Rue des Morillons, 75732 Paris; tel. (1) 45 31 14 80.

TRAVELLERS WITH DISABILITIES

Paris was not planned with the disabled traveller in mind, though things are steadily improving: the Louvre, for instance, has several lifts (elevators) and can suggest special tours designed to ease getting round the museum. Airports are equipped to help; for Orly South telephone (1) 49 75 30 70 and Orly West (1) 46 75 18 18. At Charles-de-Gaulle, Air Assistance is on (1) 48 62 28 24. The métro's many stairs and few lifts make it difficult but the RATP (métro, RER and bus network) offers a *voyage accompagné* service from 8am to 8pm; someone will accompany you during your trip. Book 48 hours ahead on (1) 49 59 96 00. A similar service can be arranged with the SNCF (rail network), by telephoning the appropriate railway station. Sight-impaired travellers can obtain a Braille map of the métro from Association Valentin Haüy, 5 Rue Duroc, Paris 75007; tel. (1) 47 34 07 90. It is worth getting a copy of Access in Paris, a guidebook for people with disabilities; contact Access Project (PHSP), 39 Bradley Gardens, London W13 8HE, England.

TRAVELLING TO PARIS

By air

Scheduled flights. Paris is served by two international airports, Roissy-Charles-de-Gaulle and Orly. Average journey time between Paris and Johannesburg is 13 hours, London 1 hour, New York 7 hours (less than 4 hours by Concorde), Toronto 9 hours.

Charter flights and package tours.

From the **UK** and **Ireland**: Most tour operators charter seats on scheduled flights at a reduced price as part of a package deal which could include a weekend or a couple of weeks' stay, a simple bed and breakfast arrangement or a combined 'wine tour' and visit to Paris. Among the inclusive holiday packages are tours for visitors with a common interest, such as cookery courses, school trips or art.

However, most visitors from the UK travel to France individually, either by booking directly with a ferry operator and taking a car across, or signing up for inclusive holidays which offer fly-drive and touring or self-catering arrangements.

From **North America**: ABC (Advance Booking Charters) provide air passage only (from New York, Chicago, Los Angeles and San Francisco to Paris), but OTC (One Stop Inclusive Tour Charter) package deals include airport transfers, hotel, sightseeing and meals.

Paris is the starting point for many tours of France. Wine tasting, gourmet and cooking tours, as well as tours of the château country are included in package deals leaving from over a dozen major US and Canadian cities, usually on a seasonal basis (April to October) and for periods of one to three weeks. You can also choose from fly-drive and fly-rail schemes.

From **Australia** and **New Zealand**: Package deals for Paris are offered by certain airlines. You can also travel by independent arrangement (the usual direct economy flight with unrestricted stopovers) or go on a fly-drive arrangement.

From **South Africa**: Excursion fares and numerous package deals are available, including Paris among other European sights.

By car

Cross-channel operators offer plenty of special deals at competitive prices; a good travel agent will help you to find the suitable ferry for your destination. Dover-Calais is the shortest route and most convenient port from which to reach Paris.

Le Shuttle, the car transporter service through the Channel Tunnel, takes 35 minutes. The terminals are near Folkestone and Calais.

By bus

Regular services also operate from London to Paris via cross-channel ferries or the Channel tunnel. Numerous lines link Paris with regional cities including Bordeaux, Lyons or Nice.

By rail

All the main lines converge on Paris. On the ultra-rapid TGV trains which reach 300 km/h, reservation is compulsory. Auto-train services (*Trains Autos Couchettes*) are also available from major towns. **137**

The journey between London (Waterloo) and Paris (Gare du Nord) takes only 3 hours by Eurostar train through the Channel Tunnel. For those who arrive by ferry at the French channel ports, frequent trains run to Paris.

Tickets. Visitors from abroad can buy a *France-Vacances Spécial* pass, valid for specified periods of unlimited travel on first or second class, with reductions on the Paris transport network and one or two days' free car rental (available with first class only), depending on the type of card.

Residents of Europe can buy an *Inter-Rail* or *Inter-Rail plus* card which allows one month's unlimited second-class travel on most European rail networks. The under-26 Inter-Rail card is also available for selected zones of Europe (France, Belgium, Luxembourg and Netherlands constitute one zone). The Freedom Pass is available for travel on 3, 5 or 10 days within any month, in one or more of the 26 participating countries of Europe.

People resident outside Europe and North Africa can buy a *Eurailpass* for unlimited rail travel in 17 European countries, including France. This pass must be obtained before leaving home. Anyone under 26 qualifies for the lower-priced *Eurail Youth Pass*.

WATER
Tap water is suitable for drinking (unless marked *eau non potable*).

WEIGHTS and MEASURES
The metric system – a French invention – is universal.

Length

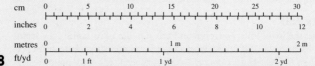

Weight

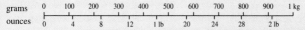

grams	0	100	200	300	400	500	600	700	800	900	1 kg
ounces	0	4	8	12	1 lb	20	24	28	2 lb		

Temperature

| °C | -30 | -25 | -20 | -15 | -10 | -5 | 0 | 5 | 10 | 15 | 20 | 25 | 30 | 35 | 40 | 45 |
| °F | | -20 | -10 | 0 | 10 | 20 | 30 | 40 | 50 | 60 | 70 | 80 | 90 | 100 | 110 | |

WOMEN TRAVELLERS

As a woman alone you should not experience more problems than in most big cities. Late night public transport should be avoided.

Budget accommodation for women can be found at the Salvation Army's Palais de la Femme, 94 Rue de Charonne, 75011; tel. (1) 43 71 11 27 and at several YWCAs (addresses from tourist offices) where the usual up-to-24 age rule does not apply in July and August.

Y

YOUTH HOSTELS *(auberges de jeunesse)*

For more information, ask for the free guide to all French Youth Hostels, obtainable from the Fédération Unie des Auberges de Jeunesse (FUAJ), 27 Rue Pajol, 75018 Paris; tel. (1) 44 89 87 27. For youth hostels in Paris, advance reservation is essential, year round.

Tourist information offices (see p.133) can give you a booklet *Jeunes à Paris* (Youth in Paris) with addresses and telephone numbers of hostels, student halls, etc. which provide accommodation. (Some cannot be reserved in advance.) The tourist offices may be able to arrange a reservation for you, but again, only on the same day.

UCRIF (Union des Centres de Rencontres Internationaux), 72 Rue Rambuteau, Paris 75001; tel. (1) 40 26 57 64, has a number of centres in Paris. Accueil des Jeunes en France, 119 Rue Saint-Martin, 75004; tel. (1) 42 77 87 80 (also in main departure hall at Gare du Nord; tel. (1) 42 85 86 19) has several hostels for young visitors. **139**

Index

Where more than one reference occurs, the one in **bold** refers to the main entry. Entries in *italics* refer to illustrations.

Other Berlitz titles include:

019/604